In a world of division, hostility, anger, and vio ache for hope. What might hope look like? Wh the people who might be hope's agents? What r

For decades now, Dr. Salim Munayer, Founder and Executive Director of Musalaha, has lived, breathed, and enacted responses to such questions. Not only that, he and those who have joined him have done so in the context of one of most intensely divided and hostile regions in the world. In Palestine, religious, political, social, and economic conflicts are rife and the mood is either hot or hotter.

This collection of essays about reconciliation couldn't be more important. They are expressions of sobering hope. These writers' voices and angles of wisdom arise from living into the fierce intersection of layered, protracted conflict, and doing so as ministers of reconciliation.

I urge you to absorb these essays, to pray that you will think carefully and critically about them, and that you will let your life and actions become manifestations of such justice, reconciliation, and hope.

Mark Labberton, PhD
President,
Fuller Theological Seminary, Pasadena, California, USA

This book is essential for any person who is interested in reconciliation, peace-building, and the Palestinian-Israeli conflict. The experience, insight, and reflection of Musalaha is relevant to any context. The concept of "stages of reconciliation," which I have used in my teaching and in my personal life, is particularly helpful. Moreover, this book truly challenges us to view the "other" in a different way, encouraging us to question our identity construction in relation to those around us. I recommend this book to anyone who wants to make a positive change to situations of conflict, be that in the Holy Land or elsewhere.

Shireen Awwad Hilal
Director of Community and Development Outreach,
Bethlehem Bible College, Palestine

The stages of reconciliation addressed in the book have been profoundly transformative in my life. From the initial exhilaration of finding brothers and sisters from "the other side," to the frustration and despair of confronting disparate narratives, the experience has been deepening and enriching, while providing a healthy dose of humility. Moreover, I have found a treasure of friends and confidants with whom I share the challenges of living within the tension of "both/and" rather than "either/or." I will go so far as to say that this journey may provide hope for our shared futures. This book is highly recommended.

Rittie Katz, MEd
Life Coach and Author
Teacher, Jerusalem Academy of Music and Dance

Journey through the Storm is a must-read for all who work for reconciliation in our troubled world. Being in the ministry of reconciliation for decades in one of the most critical areas on earth – Israel and Palestine – is a reason in itself to account for God´s blessing. The model which Musalaha developed through the years has proven to be both successful and challenging at the same time. And the experience of Musalaha generates hope at all checkpoints of conflict and war throughout the world. I hope the book will be read by many.

Johannes Reimer, DTh
Director of Peace and Reconciliation Network,
World Evangelical Alliance

Journey through the Storm

Langham
GLOBAL LIBRARY

Journey through the Storm

*Lessons from Musalaha
Ministry of Reconciliation*

Edited by

Salim J. Munayer

Langham
GLOBAL LIBRARY

© 2020 Musalaha Ministry of Reconciliation

Published 2020 by Langham Global Library
An imprint of Langham Publishing
www.langhampublishing.org

Langham Publishing and its imprints are a ministry of Langham Partnership

Langham Partnership
PO Box 296, Carlisle, Cumbria, CA3 9WZ, UK
www.langham.org

Previously published in 2018 by Musalaha Ministry of Reconciliation: ISBN 978-9-65555-549-3

ISBNs:
978-1-83973-023-8 Print
978-1-83973-024-5 ePub
978-1-83973-025-2 Mobi
978-1-83973-026-9 PDF

Salim J. Munayer hereby asserts his moral right to be identified as the Author of the General Editor's part in the Work in accordance with sections 77 and 78 of the Copyright, Designs and Patents Act 1988.

All rights reserved. No part of this publication may be reproduced, stored in a retrieval system or transmitted, in any form or by any means, electronic, mechanical, photocopying, recording or otherwise, without the prior written permission of the publisher or the Copyright Licensing Agency.

Requests to reuse content from Langham Publishing are processed through PLSclear. Please visit www.plsclear.com to complete your request.

All Scripture quotations, unless otherwise indicated, are from the Holy Bible, New International Version®, NIV®. Copyright ©1973, 1978, 1984 by Biblica, Inc.™ Used by permission of Zondervan. All rights reserved worldwide. www.zondervan.com

Scriptures labeled NKJV are from the New King James Version. Copyright © 1982 by Thomas Nelson, Inc. Used by permission. All rights reserved.

British Library Cataloguing-in-Publication Data
A catalogue record for this book is available from the British Library

ISBN: 978-1-83973-023-8

Cover & Book Design: projectluz.com

Langham Partnership actively supports theological dialogue and an author's right to publish but does not necessarily endorse the views and opinions set forth here or in works referenced within this publication, nor can we guarantee technical and grammatical correctness. Langham Partnership does not accept any responsibility or liability to persons or property as a consequence of the reading, use or interpretation of its published content.

Contents

Foreword ix
Preface xi
1 Introduction to Musalaha: A Conversation 1
　　Salim J. Munayer and Evan Thomas
2 An Interview with Salim J. Munayer 5
3 The Stages of Reconciliation 9
　　From Musalaha's *A Curriculum of Reconciliation*

Stage One: Beginning Relationships

4 Conflict 21
　　From Musalaha's *A Curriculum of Reconciliation*
5 The Voice of Vision 31
　　By Salim J. Munayer
6 The Transformative Power of Conflict 33
　　By Joshua Korn
7 Listening 37
　　From Musalaha's *A Curriculum of Reconciliation*
8 Women's Narrative: The Art of Listening 47
　　By Louise Thomsen

Stage Two: Opening Up

9 Identity in Conflict and Reconciliation...................... 53
　　From Musalaha's *A Curriculum of Reconciliation*
10 Mixing Oil and Water: A Messianic Jewish Perspective 61
　　By a Musalaha participant
11 History and Narrative 63
　　From Musalaha's *A Curriculum of Reconciliation*
12 Fellowship: Breaking the Taboo 73
　　By Salim J. Munayer
13 Obstacles to Reconciliation.................................. 77
　　From Musalaha's *A Curriculum of Reconciliation*

Stage Three: Withdrawal

14 Forgiveness 87
　　From Musalaha's *A Curriculum of Reconciliation*

15	Teaching Israelis and Palestinians Forgiveness 99
	By Salim J. Munayer
16	Fighting the Fear: What Are We So Afraid Of? 101
	By Louise Thomsen
17	Vengeance Is Mine? Breaking the Cycle of Violence 105
	By Salim J. Munayer
18	Healing Brokenness 109
	By Louise Thomsen

Stage Four: Reclaiming Identity

19	Returning to Identity 115
	From Musalaha's *A Curriculum of Reconciliation*
20	Imposing, Expressing, and Enlarging Identity 127
	By Salim J. Munayer
21	Remembering Rightly 129
	From Musalaha's *A Curriculum of Reconciliation*

Stage Five: Committing and Returning

22	Dealing with Discouragement 139
	From Musalaha's *A Curriculum of Reconciliation*
23	Patient Hope for Reconciliation 143
	By Hadassa, Musalaha Participant
24	Justice from a Biblical Perspective 145
	From Musalaha's *A Curriculum of Reconciliation*

Stage Six: Taking Steps

25	Christian Perspectives on Change: Personal and Societal Change . . 159
	By Mae Elise Cannon
26	From Arm-Wrestling to Shaking Hands 171
	By Salim J. Munayer
27	The Cross and Reconciliation 177
	By Salim J. Munayer
28	Blessing and Cursing 185
	By Salim J. Munayer

	Contributors 187
	Bibliography 189

Foreword

In the latter part of 1988, while we were studying together in a program designed to sharpen ministry skills among indigenous leaders, Salim Munayer approached me with the details of a vision he sensed God had given him. As he shared in broad strokes the biblical call for reconciliation between our two conflicted peoples, something resonated deeply. When he asked me to join him in developing the concepts into practical initiatives involving our respective faith communities, my answer was almost an immediate *yes*! Soon after, Musalaha was brought into being. A basic infrastructure was established with Salim as director, and an equal number of experienced leaders from the Palestinian Christian and Messianic Jewish communities formed a board of oversight. This same model of leadership was to quickly become the hallmark of all Musalaha initiatives.

Twenty-five years ago, the term *reconciliation* was not a central issue for the local body of Christ. The Arabic and Hebrew speaking communities enjoyed only minimal fellowship with each other. However, the challenges of the First Intifada changed everything[1] – young Messianic servicemen were embroiled in the civil unrest, and young Palestinian Christians, suffering the frustrations and indignities of checkpoints and military occupation, became involved in the resistance. The polarization between the two groups deepened, and Jesus's call to his body for unity became more and more urgent.

Musalaha responded with desert encounters – first bringing together young adults from both sides, and then older, experienced ministry leadership, both men and women. Stepping out of the comfort and safety of our homes, the harsh environment of the desert became our classroom where we faced one another (often for the first time) on level ground. These early days presented a very steep learning curve for us all as we learned to worship, study, and pray together, forming the relationships that would become a vital basis for the manifold ministries that Musalaha now represents.

The desert encounters, lasting three to five days, and the various seminars held during those first years would hone our skills at providing a safe environment where these new relationships could withstand inevitable

---

1. The First Intifada was a Palestinian uprising that began in December 1987 and ended in September 1993 with the signing of the Oslo Accords.

challenges as we attempted to deal with hard issues such as the roots of the conflict, obstacles to peace, and the theology of the land. Those who chose to persevere would form, in time, a broadening circle of leaders committed to the vision and willing to stand firm in the face of intercommunity opposition to unity and peace. People from both sides were now willing to take the courageous step from being involved in the conflict to being active in reconciliation and peacemaking. This new dynamic provided impetus for Musalaha to create a model, specifically suited to our conflict zone, for training leaders in reconciliation – and the resulting curriculum is bearing significant fruit in our and other contexts of conflict.

Youth leaders from both communities now receive high-quality professional training together. Musalaha summer camps and youth initiatives (including missions abroad) are among the best the local body has to offer. Children who have participated in the camps often return to serve as counselors, creating a healthy continuity. The women's section has grown quickly into the largest and most active department.

It has been a tremendous privilege to see Musalaha's credibility steadily develop in the eyes of the international Christian world. The testimonies of our successes (and heartbreaks) and the methodologies that have been tried and tested in the fire of one of the world's most complex conflict zones are now providing models for others. As a result, we are able to invite foreign study groups to learn from us and to raise awareness of our conflict by encouraging people to partner with us in reconciliation activities.

For all this, God alone deserves the glory as he demonstrates the power of his grace and his word to change our lives and our communities. The Middle East is volatile and the new covenant community here in Israel/Palestine is not immune to its painful struggles. Has Musalaha risen to the challenge of providing an alternative paradigm? I sincerely believe so. The fruit of these labors will lay down solid foundations for generations to come.

Evan Thomas
Chair of the Musalaha Board (1991–2019)

Preface

This is the third edition of *Journey through the Storm*, an accumulation of Musalaha's nearly thirty years of work in the field of reconciliation – thirty years during which we have accrued significant expertise with which to enrich the reconciliation journey in this land and in other regions as well. Along with personal stories and reflections, this edition also includes material from the Curriculum of Reconciliation. The full curriculum is available as *Musalaha: A Curriculum of Reconciliation*, written by Salim Munayer and published in 2014.

Throughout the years, we have developed, taught, modified, and refined our model of reconciliation within the context of the Israeli-Palestinian conflict. We have shared this curriculum in different locations around the world and found it universally applicable to different situations of ethnic conflict. The stages of reconciliation comprise the unique and personal process undergone by individuals and groups as sincere friendships are made, enmity is overcome, and controversial issues which divide communities are explored. In response to demand, we have created this condensed, easy-to-read version, which incorporates essays and reflections to accompany the reader through the stages.

Empowerment is a central element of Musalaha's methodology, and we strive to embrace a variety of different voices – male, female, Israeli, Palestinian, Jewish, Christian, Muslim. This book highlights contributions mostly from the Messianic Jewish and Palestinian Christian communities.

As a consequence of the 1948 and 1967 wars, those in the Palestinian community found themselves under different sovereignties: there are those who are citizens of the Palestinian Authority (PA), those who hold Israeli citizenship, and those who are "residents" of Israel but not citizens. Since the Oslo Accords, Palestinians in the West Bank live partially under Israeli military rule, with passports issued by the PA, while those living in Gaza, who have been under Hamas rule since 2007, also hold passports issued by the PA. While Israel withdrew unilaterally from the Gaza Strip and four settlements in Samaria in 2005, Gaza is still under siege.

Most Palestinians remaining in Israel were granted citizenship following the 1948 war but were subject to military rule until 1966, and they suffer inequality in the spheres of citizenship, property rights, education, and more. The passage of the nation-state law in 2018 created further inequalities, declaring, "The exercise of the right to national self-determination in the State of Israel is unique to the Jewish People."[1]

Following the annexation of East Jerusalem and the occupation of the West Bank and Gaza in 1967, East Jerusalem Palestinians are residents of Israel but not citizens. They have the right to vote in municipal elections but not in the Knesset. Depending on where they reside and their vocations, "Palestinian Israelis" often have daily contact with Jewish Israelis. However, the majority are separated by their neighborhoods, their communities, and their educational systems. Palestinians in the West Bank have limited if any contact with ordinary Jewish Israelis unless they have permits to work in or visit Israel.

In this book, we provided an intimate glimpse into the encounters Musalaha facilitates, striving to provide the most neutral and "equal" environment possible in order to develop trust, to address the issues, and to allow the voices which you find in this book, especially their grievances, to emerge and be heard. Musalaha hopes that the outcome of the process described here will be that some of these grievances will be addressed in a concrete manner, by means of collaborative endeavors which will impact the surrounding societies.

I would like to take this opportunity to thank Jessica White and Gilah Kahn for their work on this edition. It would not have come about without their tireless efforts.

In many ways, this new edition is an ideal introduction to Musalaha, as it presents our process of reconciliation with both the highs and lows of this journey on full display. I hope that it encourages and inspires all who read it. Jesus urges us to be peacemakers (Matt 5:9), and this work is dedicated to all who respond to his call. Whether you consider yourself an expert on the Israeli-Palestinian conflict or are just beginning to make sense of past and present events in the Holy Land, it is our sincere desire that, above all, you will experience hope and purpose as you move through our story.

Salim J. Munayer
Executive Director, Musalaha

---

1. Knesset website https://knesset.gov.il/laws/special/eng/BasicLawNationState.pdf. Unofficial translation by Dr. Susan Hattis Rolef.

1

Introduction to Musalaha: A Conversation

Salim J. Munayer and Evan Thomas

Salim: When discussing our attitudes and feelings about the conflict, the feeling of frustration immediately comes to mind. We are frustrated by the senseless loss of life and property and the indifference of each side toward the other's aspirations, suffering, and loss. Some of us are frustrated by the ease with which we may enter a cycle of revenge that harms the innocent. Despite knowing that vengeance will not resolve the conflict, many are drawn into the cycle of retaliation which is difficult to break.
Evan: Rather than frustration, my overriding emotions following these years of escalating conflict are sadness and disillusionment.

I guess I had hoped beyond reason that our peoples would choose peaceful solutions to the enormous problems we face. It has been heartbreaking to see the effect on the people of my city. A few years ago, there was a high degree of mobility (for business and social reasons) between Netanya and the large West Bank towns that are only fourteen kilometers away. Since October 2000, and the beginning of the intifada, our communities have been open in their hatred and fear of one another. We are now separated by a huge concrete wall, and this open hatred and fear of one another has continued to this present day.

My family and I used to regularly visit Palestinian Christian friends in the West Bank. They too would visit us, and we spent weekends in one another's homes. It is now very difficult and often impossible to do so due to security considerations. We still cherish the friendships, but an enormous effort is required to maintain them. It's just not the same.

Salim: Yes, in this situation we experience a strong sense of powerlessness. We see wave after wave of events that, as individuals, we cannot control, so we feel powerless to change the situation. We are overwhelmed by the rise of hatred and dehumanization on both sides. The main area where we can hope to have an impact is in people's hearts, by challenging their attitudes toward each other. However, sometimes we feel that we take one step to reduce the violence and come to a resolution, and then events generated by governments or individuals take us many steps backward.

Evan: Like you Salim, I too struggle with a sense of powerlessness to affect the situation. I truly believe in the power of prayer, and I continually encourage my community to exercise faith that peace will be achieved between our societies. It doesn't seem like God is in too much of a hurry to answer those prayers. The reality I have to live with is a visible deepening of the rift and a future of further bloodshed – not only for us but for our kids too. At nearly fourteen, my daughter is already questioning whether she has a future here. That's tough for parents who immigrated to Israel twenty-one years ago full of idealism and hope.

Salim: The impact on our children and our hopes for the future is great. My sons attend school in downtown Jerusalem where several acts of terrorism have occurred. Both a child and a worker from their school were killed riding buses. On the other side, in Bethlehem, we have friends who have suffered greatly due to the military incursions. Most of us, as you mentioned, Evan, are greatly concerned for our children and their futures.

We are frustrated that our leaders cannot arrive at a resolution. Many Israelis and Palestinians know what is required to reach an agreement but are not willing to pay the price to achieve a compromise. The deep level of mistrust between the two sides hampers any progress in resolving these issues.

Another factor threatening any possibility of a solution is the presence of very strong, sometimes militant, minorities in both communities that do not support peaceful co-existence. The extremes are paralyzing both peoples and could lead, in the worst scenario, to a civil war. It is also frustrating that the politicians, who know what is required, are unable to make the decisions to implement change. To remain in power, they foster hatred toward other communities.

Evan: I have long ago given up any illusions of seeing effective political leadership. I agree that the destruction of trust has made it almost impossible for our leaders to make progress toward peace, despite clearly seeing what is required. However, I think there are other factors too, such as the self-serving nature of our politicians and the interference of American and European foreign policy. I am convinced that we must put our trust in a higher power. Salim, our long-term friendship and walking closely together, believing in the Musalaha vision, have taught us that. Think back on all the lives that have been affected for good. Time and again we have seen God faithfully change both Israeli and Palestinian hearts despite continuing atrocities and political rhetoric.

Salim: It has been encouraging to see believers building relationships and reaching out across the divide. I agree that the unity of the body of the Messiah is a major step toward reconciliation in a very challenging time.

When we started reconciliation meetings with Palestinian and Israeli believers at the beginning of the First Intifada, there was great disappointment in discovering that many from both sides identified so strongly with their ethnic group. Many times this reached the level of compromising biblical principles about God's love for all, as they allowed their hearts to be colored by dehumanization of the other and the expression of hatred and indifference. Palestinian Christians and Messianic Jews have a need to prove their ethnic loyalties because they are both minorities in their own communities and are perceived with suspicion. Therefore, some make statements of loyalty to their ethnic group which can be aggressive or hurtful toward believers from the other side. Some discount each other's loyalty to God and question their theological position. They refuse to meet and fellowship with other believers unless they affirm certain theological or political positions. This can even reach the point of discouraging supporters from partnering with local ministries from the other side.

Evan: One of the motivating forces behind my commitment to the Musalaha vision of biblical reconciliation is the degree of polarization I see demonstrated by the church worldwide. It seems that any Christian with an interest in Israel or the Jewish or Arab peoples suddenly sees him or herself as a Middle East expert. The theologies of entire Christian movements have been influencing our respective constituencies for too long. Instead of contributing to an atmosphere of reconciliation and supporting the Palestinian Christian and Messianic Jewish communities in our stand for the gospel, they have all-too-often reinforced the polarization we suffer from.

It is time for us to take a strong position regarding our mutual identity in the Messiah despite our differences in eschatology. God knows, my ethnic identity is very important to me, as it is very important to me to be able to express my faith in Yeshua (Jesus) in the context of my Jewish identity. Within this context lies also my strong loyalty to my people, group, and nation; however, this is not at the expense of my loyalty to the community of faith that is inclusive of us both. We must live with this enormous tension, but with God's help we can make a difference. The countless testimonies we have been witness to take this way beyond philosophy.

Salim: Yes, we have seen many believers from both sides rising to follow the teaching of Jesus about loving their neighbors and loving their enemies as an indication of their love to God (1 John 4:21). Many are inspired by the actions of Jesus on the cross, reconciling us to God and to each other, fulfilling what Paul taught in Ephesians 2 about the wall of hatred and enmity. Through the years of Musalaha, ever greater numbers of believers from both sides have chosen, in an act of obedience, a path of reconciliation in the midst of conflict and division.

Evan: Salim, you and I have been accused many times of operating on a mere humanistic level lacking in real spiritual understanding. I certainly don't claim to be a "spiritual giant," but the only thing I am convinced of is that Yeshua accomplished on the cross something that no human endeavor ever could. I am convinced that we are on the right track. Every success of intercommunity fellowship, no matter how insignificant it may seem, is a statement about the truth of the gospel. Every time we express our love for one another's communities, we demonstrate the Messiah's love for humanity.

I count it a real victory this year to see Arab Christian pastors for the first time being lovingly included in the Israeli Messianic leaders' retreat movement. Their testimony in our midst was such a mutual encouragement. We have much to celebrate – look at how God is causing our congregations to flourish despite the social and economic conditions that surround us. We have much to be thankful for!

2

An Interview with Salim J. Munayer

I would like to hear more about Musalaha activities. What do the young people who participate in your programs learn when they listen to one another in the desert?

Salim: The most important aspect of a Musalaha activity is the exposure to the "other." This is true for children through to adults. All age demographics are constantly bombarded by negative (mis)information about people from the other side of the conflict, by schools and the media, and even via discussions among family and friends.

This inundation leads to most Israelis and Palestinians perceiving each other as enemies by default, and the conflict as a force of nature. Their enmity is seen to be as natural as the struggle between dog and cat or cat and mouse. This naturally leads to fear of the other, bitterness, and even hatred. But it also leads to resignation and hopelessness.

While meeting with people from the other side is a good antidote for anyone living with this fear and bitterness, often the greater success rate, in terms of changing attitudes, is found among children and youth who are more flexible and less set in their ways than their older counterparts. They are able to listen objectively without becoming instantly defensive. This is not to say that it is an easy road to walk for the youth, but it is easier.

Whenever Palestinians and Israelis meet, they discover that on a personal level they can relate to each other as they are actually quite similar. They see that the "others" are not all monsters, contrary to what they may have been led to believe. The problem is that in their everyday lives, many have no opportunity to meet the other, except at checkpoints. So they begin to believe the lies they are told. The sooner you counteract the negativity created through ignorance, the easier it is for them to recognize the truth and be set free. The way forward is to break the cycle of dehumanization and stereotyping. Once we learn to see each other as humans, this becomes possible. Meeting with each other face to face is the best option, and therefore Musalaha provides a setting in which that type of meeting can take place.

Musalaha has been working in reconciliation since 1990. Looking back, can you tell us about the long-term impact of reconciliation?

Salim: Musalaha's reconciliation activities have a huge impact. They can totally change a person's perception and completely alter their understanding of the conflict. Relationships with people from the other side are established over time. This is something that, unfortunately, makes our participants unique in both Israeli and Palestinian societies. But it also serves as a testimony to the sincerity of the reconciliation that takes place. These friendships do not end after the activity is over but last for years.

Once friendships are built, and the lies of stereotypes and dehumanization have been exposed, participants can begin to work toward joint goals that benefit both communities, such as peace and social justice. The work of Musalaha and other organizations which focus on reconciliation has helped to create a shift in the thinking of the body of the Messiah. Twenty years ago, reconciliation was not on the agenda. Now every ministry in the land is involved with reconciliation between Palestinians and Israelis in some way, even those who are theologically opposed. We have seen an increase in the willingness of people to put themselves on the line and pay a price for peace and reconciliation. People formerly antagonistic to Musalaha and its message of reconciliation have become Musalaha leaders, and the principles learned through reconciliation training have been applied to contexts outside of the Israeli-Palestinian conflict. Everywhere, from the congregation to the home, dealing with conflict in a healthy, Christ-centered way is useful.

Over the years, I have been blessed by the opportunity to see many participants in Musalaha's activities changed by the message of hope through reconciliation, and I have seen them take this message with them to other ministries and even other countries. A number of Musalaha participants have undergone the stages of the reconciliation process and become leaders of reconciliation-focused activities with Musalaha and other ministries. The progress these young leaders have made, by first participating as a youth or young adult, and later leading youth or young adult activities, is especially encouraging.

Our children's camps started five years ago, and it is very exciting to see the leaders who were once campers and are now familiar with the work of reconciliation. We see the same phenomenon where those who were once participants in our young adult program are now leading the process. We are excited to see how their generation will affect the future, confident that they will heal hurts since they have a head start in understanding and caring for each other.

Can you share a personal story or anecdote that might help our readers to understand the significance of your work?

Salim: The following story of an Israeli woman reflects the slow, at times painful, yet ultimately rewarding process of reconciliation.

This woman remembers hearing stories of Israeli brutality during the First Intifada (the Palestinian uprising which lasted from 1987 to 1993) and making a conscious decision to ignore them. It was too difficult to deal with at the time, and contradicted what she heard from the Israeli media, which she trusted. So she chose to ignore the truth. Even when she heard Palestinian Christians, fellow believers in Jesus the Messiah, describing their treatment at the hands of Israeli soldiers, she rejected their stories as impossible, and remembers hiding in a restroom during a conference to avoid having to hear them.

While working through the anger and blame that she felt about what the Israelis suffered during the conflict, she came to realize that her anger, along with the misinformation she was hearing, were preventing her from seeing any guilt in her attitude or in the actions of the Israelis. She recognized that she was blinded and that she was the cause of her own blindness, realizing that she would never be able to forgive and be forgiven unless she sought the truth, whatever the cost. This conviction led her to become involved with Musalaha. Her strong testimony, and willingness to boldly share with others and deal with the controversial issues, has been a great blessing to Musalaha and to other participants. The change in her life was brought about by God, not humans, and God is seen through her words and actions.

How can Christians around the world contribute to the work of reconciliation and peacebuilding in the Middle East from within our own context?

Salim: Christians can and should remain informed about the positive developments emerging from the Palestinian-Israeli conflict. It is easy to become discouraged because the news is usually bad. However, there is much reconciliation activity and many things to be thankful for. You must fight the myth that there is no solution to the Israeli-Palestinian conflict. We *know* the solution and we *have* the solution. However difficult it may be, reconciliation is the only way. It is far preferable to continued violence and hate.

It is important to support these reconciliation efforts financially and with prayer. Without support and prayer, Musalaha's projects, which bring Israelis and Palestinians together, would not be possible, and they would be unable to meet, learn from one another, and learn to love each other as God commands them to. The global church is already a part of the conflict. Will it remain part of the conflict, or will it become part of the solution? Apathy or willful ignorance will only contribute to the conflict, whereas seeking the truth, justice, and God's will can only further the cause of reconciliation and peace.

Any other words you'd like to share with the church?

Salim: Thank you again for all your support and prayer. Please do not stop, and please know that we keep you in our prayers as well. Also, remember the power of the cross and the resurrection. That power is evident when we find, as we do here, people so filled with bitterness and hate who learn to love each other through reconciliation. This is only possible through God and his ultimate expression of love through the sacrifice of the cross. God is working powerfully in the lives of Israeli and Palestinian believers. This is not something the rest of the Christian community can afford to miss.

3

The Stages of Reconciliation

From Musalaha's *A Curriculum of Reconciliation*

Musalaha and other organizations involved in peace work and reconciliation have noted a number of recurring phenomena when Palestinians and Israelis encounter one another and begin the journey of reconciliation. Often, we are drawn together out of curiosity and the desire to meet the other. As we are in conflict, we do not arrive at an encounter simply as individuals. We come as parts and representatives of our respective communities, and carry with us the pain, demonization, dehumanization, and struggles our peoples suffer and project on each other.

Some approaches to communities in conflict focus on individuals and building personal relationships, hoping there will be a ripple effect. Others advocate focusing on group dynamics, arguing that our conflict is not about individuals, but about two identities or nations.[1] Musalaha attempts to combine these approaches, encouraging participants to focus on relating as individuals (the interpersonal approach), while also encouraging them to relate to each other as members of specific groups or peoples (the intergroup approach).[2]

A policy of separation is prevalent in both Israeli and Palestinian societies. For the most part, the interaction between our two peoples is limited, and most social,cultural, and educational initiatives take place within our respective separate communities. There is little opportunity for relationship-building, and one of the few ways people from both sides can speak to each other and

---

1. Hanafi, "Dancing Tango during Peacebuilding," 69. See also Halabi and Sonnenschein, "School for Peace," 278–279.
2. Doubilet, "Coming Together," 52.

develop relationships is through people-to-people encounters initiated by reconciliation and peace organizations.

Additionally, a severe imbalance of power exists between us. Israel has a state and a developed military and is in control of the country as well as the lives of many Palestinians. The Palestinians have no state, no military, and their political situation and even daily activities are often subject to Israel's control. Through our encounters, we see how this imbalance manifests itself in our group identities, and we become more aware of how our culture and education reinforce it. One of the challenges in bringing people together is attempting to counter this imbalance.

Reconciliation is not an event or even a linear sequence of activities but rather a somewhat cyclical and chaotic process that takes place in stages and is never-ending.[3] This process is fluid, and each individual progresses at his or her own pace. We encourage groups and individuals to proceed slowly and steadily, as attempts to speed up the process often fail. Throughout Musalaha's thirty years of experience, we have noticed certain dynamics which repeat themselves. We call these the stages of reconciliation.

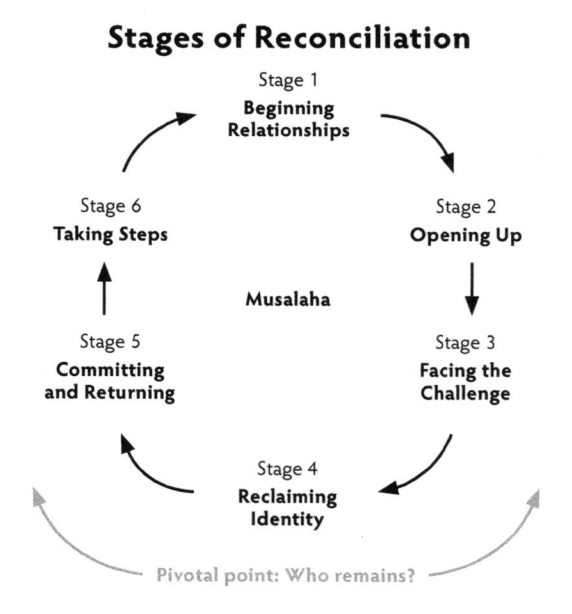

Stages of Reconciliation

Stage 1
Beginning Relationships

Stage 2
Opening Up

Stage 3
Facing the Challenge

Stage 4
Reclaiming Identity

Stage 5
Committing and Returning

Stage 6
Taking Steps

Musalaha

Pivotal point: Who remains?

---

3. Kraybill, "Cycle of Reconciliation," 73. See also Steinberg and Bar-On, "Dialogue," 148.

Stage One: Beginning Relationships

Musalaha tries to offset the imbalance of power by bringing together an equal number of Palestinians and Israelis for a few days in a neutral location, such as the desert or a locale abroad. Since we try to foster both interpersonal and intergroup relationships, we have found it beneficial to work with smaller groups, usually numbering no more than thirty people in total. Generally, our women's and family groups meet abroad, while our youth, young adult, and community leader groups meet in the desert. On these trips participants are isolated, far from civilization and also from security personnel, checkpoints, and manifestations of our conflict.

In the desert, we are forced to depend on one another and to work together as we engage in discussions, teachings, and challenging physical activities. In the stillness, we can shake off the policy of separation and forge meaningful relationships while participating in non-threatening activities. The unique atmosphere of these trips expedites the breaking down of the dehumanization and demonization which characterizes both sides. While in the desert, our groups learn about the Musalaha method and participate in interactive workshops where they can safely discuss the issues we raise. These are combined with outings and relationship-building activities, which aid in the fostering of meaningful interaction during this first stage.

As much as possible we speak in both Hebrew and Arabic, since this is often the first time participants have heard the language of the other (sometimes considered "the enemy") in a positive context. Through joint activities we begin to trust one another and feel more comfortable about taking risks and sharing information about ourselves, sharing resources, and showing vulnerability.

During this initial stage, we emphasize our commonalities, particularly the values or beliefs we share. These provide an overarching common framework in which we feel comfortable opening up. While we touch on the conflict, at this stage we tend to avoid addressing the more volatile political issues and encourage people to share their feelings and listen to each other's fears, suffering, and experiences. We focus on establishing the relationships which enable participants to continue on the journey of reconciliation.

In our experience, when Israelis and Palestinians first come together, they are excited and enthusiastic. One of the primary motivations is simple curiosity. Participants also view the encounters as fun and adventurous social opportunities. Both during and following a Musalaha encounter we see an increase in the social acceptance of the other, primarily on an interpersonal level but also (to a lesser extent) on an intergroup level. On our last evening together many express feelings and opinions that indicate that prejudice and hostility toward the other have decreased. We also discuss what we have learned and accomplished and encourage people to remain in contact in the future.

During this first stage, we teach units on conflict, Musalaha's stages of reconciliation, the Biblical principles of reconciliation, and listening. Since, in addition to being fulfilling and meaningful, the journey of reconciliation is also painful and sometimes demanding, it is important for participants to know that feelings of hesitation, caution, excitement, fear, and pain are all part of this normal and natural process. Should something traumatic occur in subsequent meetings, we often return to the unit about the stages of reconciliation to remind participants that this is not a setback but rather a natural reaction within the process, so they are reassured.

Stage Two: Opening Up

Following several encounters, Israelis and Palestinians return home to their separated societies. It is not easy for them to continue their face-to-face relationships as it is often very difficult for them to meet. Israelis are not allowed to enter the area of the Palestinian Authority, and many Palestinians are only permitted to enter Israel for one or two short periods every year. Research has shown that bringing Israelis and Palestinians together for a meaningful encounter reduces social distance and lack of acceptance. However, research has also demonstrated that a one-time meeting and its benefits are not sustainable without continued face-to-face meetings and encouragement to maintain relationships.[4] Since Musalaha does not wish to lose the positive momentum of its initial encounters, and because our aim is to encourage people to journey toward reconciliation together, we provide further opportunities for encounters through follow-up activities. Our follow-ups enable participants to continue to develop their interpersonal relationships and to take part in intergroup activities.

During this stage, we once again emphasize the importance of listening to one another, and we continue to encourage relationships with trust-building activities. As participants have had time to develop relationships and are aware of their commonalities, they feel more comfortable being open with each other and expressing their differences. At this point, the Palestinians feel comfortable enough to be forthcoming about their grievances, and Israelis may be overwhelmed by the stories and political opinions expressed. The Israelis' shock at the breadth of accusations and complaints is often the result of the

---

4. Kupermintz and Saloman, "Lessons to Be Learned," 295.

limited interaction with and understanding of Palestinians' lives. Additional subjects explored during Stage Two emphasize conflicting points of view in the contexts of the topics we cover. The units are titled as follows: "Identity," "Approaches to Conflict," "History and Narrative," "Obstacles to Reconciliation," and "Theological Differences: The Implication of Theology on Others."

During this stage many experience surprise, loss of self-esteem, vulnerability, and fear that the risks they have taken may be rewarded with harm as their personal and group identities are challenged or attacked. Often this results in participants' desire to focus on commonalities rather than contend with some of the more difficult aspects of reconciliation. Our response is to remind them of the stages they must experience, and the fact that they are in the midst of a process and there can be no progress or reconciliation if one refuses to face the pain inherent in the conflict. During the first and second stages, Israelis often find it easier to express differing and contradictory opinions, whereas the Palestinian side tends to present itself as a united front, apparently in an attempt to strengthen their side and rectify the imbalance of power.

We have seen that Stages One and Two overlap to some extent and also that younger groups are able and willing to proceed at a faster pace. During this stage we organize numerous follow-ups to promote further relationship-building and more discussion about issues which divide the two sides.

Stage Three: Withdrawal

Musalaha and other organizations have noted that following the initial positive contact with the other, participants often experience a period of withdrawal or regression.[5] This is generally because the issues raised during Stage Two may challenge participants' perception of the conflict or their own identity. Again, a degree of withdrawal is part of the process. We remind participants that "the goal is not to avoid pain, but rather to persist in the never-ending work of self-definition and negotiation required to transform the differences that exist in any relationship from liabilities into assets."[6]

Despite our warning of this possibility during the initial encounter, it is always a shock to be challenged and find oneself wanting to step back. It is often at this point that the Israelis begin to discuss their grievances, as both

---

5. Steinberg and Bar-On, "Dialogue," 148–149.
6. Kraybill, "Cycle of Reconciliation," 78.

sides continue the discussion about identity. Activities are then focused on the topics of power, forgiveness, and dealing with psychological trauma.

Sometimes the hurt experienced causes the relationships to fade. Participants may argue passionately about their political opinions, theological views, or historical narratives. Both sides may feel as though their suspicions have been confirmed and surrender to the self-fulfilling prophecy that discord is inevitable, that their differences simply cannot be bridged.

Withdrawal, whether emotional or physical, is a natural and healthy response to injury. Depending on how it is approached, it can lead to bitterness and even more deeply entrenched prejudice or to introspection and the reclaiming of identity (Stage Four). The length of the withdrawal period varies. In our experience, some participants may choose not to attend follow-up events for a year or even longer. Some abandon the process altogether.

Stage Four: Reclaiming Identity

During this period of withdrawal, participants may reflect on identity individually or as a group. Both individual participant's self-esteem and the group confidence have been challenged, which seems to prove that identity is one of the first casualties of painful conflict.[7] Christian author and expert on peace-building and reconciliation, John Paul Lederach, notes, "The journey through conflict toward reconciliation always involves turning to face oneself. Jacob has to face his fear. To turn toward his brother, his enemy, he first has to deal with himself, his fears, and his past actions."[8]

In Stage Four, we encourage participants to be aware of their feelings and to accept their sense of hurt. We discuss topics such as reclaiming identity, remembering rightly, and election, covenant, and sovereignty. We also encourage affirmation of participants' respective identities, as denial of a person's identity will not lead to genuine reconciliation. We attempt to affirm participants' pride in belonging to a group, although this may have negative manifestations if this belonging is at the expense of the other or antagonistic towards the other. At this difficult stage people often feel stuck, distant, and sometimes bitter, defeated, or frustrated. Once again, we remind participants about the stages of reconciliation and that these feelings are a natural part of the process.

---

7. Kraybill, 75.
8. Lederach, *Journey Toward Reconciliation*, 23.

Musalaha stresses that embracing the other should not come at the expense of one's own ethnic or spiritual identity. Those who fully engage with this stage and continue to be involved in the process despite the difficulties they encounter often discover they are more secure in their own identity. At this stage participants are compelled to make a choice, as individuals and as part of a group, and this is a pivotal point in the stages of reconciliation.

Pivotal Point: Who Remains?

At this crucial juncture, participants decide whether to continue with the journey of reconciliation or to opt out. Some choose to return to their previous theological, political, and cultural positions and prejudices. Those who persist often make a conscious choice to continue despite the challenges and carry on with a new openness and vulnerability. This pivotal point usually occurs between Stages Three and Five.

Stage Five: Committing and Returning

Following the decision to continue, after contending with the challenge to identity within the context of the group relationship, participants continue to Stage Five. Now they commit to the process, prepared to take risks to deepen relationship building. Since the relationships have been built gradually, participants have a firm foundation from which to continue to engage with critical issues related to the conflict. During this stage, participants are able to listen to each other's grievances in the context of a relationship, without becoming defensive. Due to the maturity that has developed throughout the process, they understand that both sides have legitimate grievances, and recognize and accept one another without feeling threatened. At this point participants are usually willing to acknowledge their own shortcomings as they have gained insight into how their own group has contributed to the problems and violence between the two sides. As trust is built it becomes easier and less painful to make progress.

In intractable conflicts there are no quick fixes, and it is easy to feel discouraged by the lack of progress in our societies. For this reason, we teach methods to deal with discouragement resulting from the hard work of developing and maintaining unity. This is also the stage where we introduce the essential issue of biblical justice. One verse we emphasize is "Mercy and truth have met together; righteousness and peace have kissed" (Ps 85:10 NKJV). Musalaha believes that justice can only be effective when each of the following four elements is present – mercy, truth, justice (righteousness), and peace. Justice without mercy leads to further injustice. It is impossible to achieve justice without addressing the truth. And where is the virtue of justice if it does not bring peace? In addition to the teachings about discouragement, this stage also marks the introduction of justice from a biblical perspective and the theology of reconciliation.

Stage Six: Taking Steps

As a result of mutual recognition and commitment to one another and to reconciliation, participants are now willing to take steps to correct and restore their relationship and rectify damage committed by their respective peoples. During this stage, Israelis and Palestinians are more open about confessing their part in the conflict, asking forgiveness from one another, and taking action together and within their respective communities. This manifests itself through advocacy, joint projects, and continued involvement in the reconciliation process.

In this final stage, participants who have been perpetrators of violence or who had previously been mired in bitterness as a result of the conflict often feel liberated from guilt. Participants who have viewed themselves as victims can now relinquish blame. Both sides believe that issues have been considered and addressed within the context of their relationship and feel comfortable enough to return to their societies and begin advocating the very process they have undergone. Participants become leaders who take others on the journey of reconciliation.

To equip participants with the knowledge and tools necessary to bring these principles to their societies, we include sessions titled "Justice and Reconciliation," "Group Facilitation," and "A Christian Perspective on Change: Personal and Societal Transformation." Participants realize that the process has really only just begun as they work together to bring a message of reconciliation to their people.

Conclusion

As participants develop leadership skills through their involvement with Musalaha's program, they continually experience the stages of reconciliation but their experience deepens over time. Issues that were painful the first time around become less painful, and it is a sign of maturity that, when a participant withdraws from a painful experience, the withdrawal period is shorter.

Although we repeat the stages of reconciliation throughout the process, it is only in hindsight that new participants understand what they have experienced, for the pain is always shocking, difficult, and challenging. When participants experience the process a second time, they are more attuned to it. Musalaha's goal is to influence participants to be advocates for one another, agents of change within their societies, and leaders in their respective communities.

Stage One

Beginning Relationships

4

Conflict

From Musalaha's *A Curriculum of Reconciliation*

What Is Conflict?

Conflict is most easily defined as disagreement between people which may be expressed in various ways. In our daily lives it ranges from arguments with friends and family to the violence of crime and war. The scale of conflict may vary (an argument with a partner versus a war between two countries), and the form of a conflict may be more or less intense (a war of bullets and bombs versus a war of words), but the element of disagreement is always present.

However, conflict is not necessarily a bad thing. Christian theologian David Augsburger writes, "Conflict is essential to, ineradicable from, and inevitable in human life."[1] There is great potential for disaster as a result of conflict, but the potential for positive change is there as well; it depends on what we do. First, we examine how conflict develops, how it can change from interpersonal conflict to intergroup conflict, and especially how intergroup conflict can expand into a protracted or intractable conflict. We then briefly focus on how conflict can be transformed into something positive.

Conflict is an inevitable, inescapable part of life, which occurs wherever there is human interaction. Conflict theorists have identified the "same versus other" paradigm which leads to conflict. Encounters with others may lead to conflict if the differences between us make us uncomfortable. These differences may be in skin color, religious beliefs, or political views. Since we are all unique, these differences are to be expected, yet most people tend to instinctively

---

1. Augsburger, *Conflict Mediation across Cultures*, 5.

gravitate toward those who are similar to them. Another source of conflict is often competition for the same rights and resources.

Human subjectivity is yet another explanation for conflict. Each person views the world from his or her individual perspective and assumes it is the "right" one and that anyone who disagrees with it is wrong. This clash of "truths" or opinions often gives rise to conflict, for something that one person holds to be true and self-evident may seem completely false to someone else. In many cases, the more strongly people believe that they are right, the more likely they are to try to impose their views on others. This is true of individuals as well as societies.[2]

Intergroup Conflict

Conflicts occur on different levels, and interpersonal conflict is the most frequently encountered. A normal part of our daily lives, this type of conflict includes disagreements with a life partner, relatives, friends, or co-workers. Such conflicts are very important to the people involved but less relevant to others. They can feel intense when we are experiencing them and can be very destructive on a small scale, but intergroup conflict is potentially more dangerous because a much larger number of people is involved. The intensity and level of potential destructiveness characterizing a conflict depend on the number of people affected and usually increase as a conflict becomes more communal and less personal. The dynamics of interpersonal conflict are also present in intergroup conflict, although in the latter they tend to be amplified.

Of the many sources of intergroup conflict, we focus on two of the most common. First, we find that *conflict is made communal* because of the "us versus them" attitude. There is power in numbers. People naturally seek the protection and acceptance of a group with which they identify – for example, with a religion, ethnicity, tribe, or geographic location. This is where the "same versus other" dynamic comes into play in a communal setting. Rather than regard with hostility someone who is different from "me," we feel antagonism toward those who are different from "us."

This phenomenon has been described as a "reverse refrigerator." Normally a refrigerator cools everything inside it, and as a result emits heat to the outside world. Identifying with a group creates inner warmth, and everyone within the group benefits from that heat. However, because of the inner heat, cold

---

2. Both of these reasons are suggested and elaborated on by Augsburger, *Conflict Mediation Across Cultures*, 16–18.

exclusion is emitted to those outside the group. First, in-group love develops ("we are great"), which leads to competition and comparison ("we are better"), and eventually to out-group hatred ("we are the best"). It becomes easy to stereotype the other which allows "us" to justify however we decide to treat "them."[3]

The second source of intergroup conflict we highlight is conflict based on needs, defined as things necessary to enable us to lead normal, well-adjusted, and healthy lives. Many of these needs are related to our identity and our collective beliefs, values, culture, history, and spirituality. *When we feel that any of our personal or group needs are denied, we tend to fight for them.* This is a basic human reaction which leads to the development of intergroup conflict, especially among groups of people who are oppressed.

A sociological principle called Simmel's Rule, based on the findings of George Simmel, states, "Internal cohesion of a group is contingent on the strength of external pressure."[4] This pressure may challenge or deny our needs, and since each need is an essential part of who we are, when a need is denied or ignored, we react as individuals or as a group. The following are examples of some of these needs:[5]

1. *The need for meaning.* This is defined as how we understand the world based on our insight into and comprehension of basic principles such as justice, truth, and value. This is our paradigm, and we all seek to have our paradigms validated, which happens when we meet others who share the same one. However, too often when we encounter those with a different understanding of the world, we feel threatened. This can lead to anger, triggered when competing forms of meaning challenge our own. In the context of the Israeli-Palestinian conflict, this clash is expressed in political, ideological, and religious division and is the source of anger on both sides.

2. *The need for connectedness.* This is our sense of belonging or community, expressed through language, tribe, religion, etc. We all have a basic longing to belong, to be with "our" people who understand us and speak our language. Connectedness also refers to a feeling of attachment to a piece of land and encompasses

---

3. This dynamic is covered by Lederach, *Building Peace*, 13. Also, Brewer, "Ingroup Identification," 24–30.
4. Eriksen, "Ethnic Identity," 63.
5. This list is adapted from Redkop, *From Violence to Blessing*, 31–54.

both symbolic and physical aspects. When this connectedness is denied, we feel loneliness, alienation, and most of all, sadness. We feel disconnected from our culture and our people. Both Israelis and Palestinians have a strong sense of connectedness and national identity. Both have a strong attachment to the same land, which is the crux of the conflict and explains why, in both narratives, the themes of diaspora and exile are so significant.

3. *The need for security*. This refers to our physical security, and a guarantee of our basic human rights, which include emotional, spiritual, and economic security. This need is so important that even the threat of its denial is extremely painful and can lead to panic or violence. The feeling of security is also closely related to connectedness, since being with people who share our language, experience, culture, or religion provides a sense of security or strength in numbers. When our sense of security is denied or threatened, we feel fear, which has long-lasting emotional and psychological effects on individuals and groups. Fear paralyzes people and prevents them from living normal lives. The security of both Israelis and Palestinians is regularly threatened, and fear has become part of daily life for both peoples. Israelis fear terrorist attacks at home and abroad, while Palestinians fear the Israeli military, as well as discrimination from Israeli authorities.

4. *The need for action*. This is our feeling of being in control, and/or in charge of our environment. We need to have the ability to take action, and the power, autonomy, and agency to develop and fulfill our potential. Action also encompasses the ability to make choices and the assumption that choices are available, ranging from freedom of movement to educational and occupational possibilities. When the possibility of action is denied, and power, autonomy, and agency are limited, people feel depressed and often lose motivation. Depression may be either the cause or the result of inaction. Due to their superior military strength, Israelis are in control. However, Israelis also experience travel restrictions, international boycotts, negative world opinion, and the fear of terror attacks. Both sides feel that unsympathetic external forces control what they do, how they behave, and how they defend themselves.

5. *The need for recognition*. Everyone needs to be recognized, acknowledged, and appreciated. This need is tied to our dignity,

legitimacy, and sense of self-worth, and we are dependent on others to fulfill it. We all have a particular way of seeing ourselves, as individuals or as groups, and when challenged by a different view or by a competing claim to the title we have given ourselves, conflict can occur. We feel hurt and insulted when we are not recognized, which quickly leads to anger and even violence. This is a key issue for Israelis and Palestinians, both of whom see themselves as the sole victims of the conflict, thereby denying the suffering of the other. Both sides consistently deny each other recognition, and understandably so. If Israelis accept that in 1948 they attacked innocent, unarmed Palestinians and drove them from their homes, the ensuing sense of shame and guilt will be overwhelming. If Palestinians recognize the pain and suffering they have caused Israelis through terrorist attacks, they will also experience guilt and shame.

We may have a healthy, well-developed sense of *being/self* if our feelings of meaning, connectedness, security, recognition, and action are acknowledged, buoying our self-esteem and self-worth. These needs are just as essential to understanding conflict as they are to facilitating conflict resolution and transformation. Awareness of the issues behind the conflict helps us to resolve it.

From Intergroup Conflict to Intractable Conflict

When an intergroup conflict has continued for a long time and is seemingly impossible to resolve, we refer to it as intractable. All conflicts have the potential to develop along destructive and dangerous lines, and intractable or protracted conflicts are the most likely to assume these characteristics. The longer they last, the more likely they are to become violent, and the harder it becomes to resolve them. Although each conflict is unique, intractable conflicts seem to share certain characteristics. In identifying them, we can better understand why they seem so impossible to overcome, and we can develop methods to meet the challenges they present head on.[6]

One fundamental cause of intergroup conflict is *competition over resources*, which is related to the denial of human needs. When one group denies another group what it needs because it is in competition with it, conflict is unavoidable.

---

6. The following discussion of the characteristics of an intractable conflict draws on a number of different sources, including Redkop, *From Violence to Blessing*; Kupermintz and Saloman, "Lessons to Be Learned"; Augsburger, *Conflict Mediation across Culture*; Ashmore, Jussim, and Wilder, *Social Identity*; and Lederach, *Building Peace*.

Generally, the scarcer the resources, the more intense and protracted is the conflict. And when competition is over basic resources, the conflict is likely to become intractable. Basic needs may comprise food, water, land, or less tangible necessities, such as recognition, legitimacy, or validation of historical narrative.

In the context of the Israeli-Palestinian conflict, on the most basic level the conflict is over tangible resources such as land and water, centering on contesting claims and answers to questions such as who will control the land, who will own it, who will live on it, and who will have access to the limited supply of water? This fierce competition is also over equally significant resources such as the support of the international community, recognition of the right to self-determination, and historical legitimacy as a people.

The development of a *zero-sum mentality* on both sides – the perspective which leads people to think only in terms of black and white – also contributes to making a conflict intractable. This either/or perspective is a natural outcome of competition over resources. We fight with much more conviction if we really believe that we are in a fight to the death – a fight on which our survival is dependent – and that if they win, we lose.

When both sides view legitimacy and identity as mutually exclusive, it seems impossible to resolve a conflict in which "each identity gains some of its strength and legitimacy from negating and delegitimizing the other."[7] Many Israelis refuse to admit that the Palestinian people exist, while many Palestinians claim that Jewish people belong to the Jewish religion and are not a people with a historic connection to the land. Both sides believe that if they recognize the other's identity, then they must also recognize their claim to the land. A zero-sum mentality leaves no room for competing claims or for sharing.

The path to intractable conflict usually steers both sides toward *stereotyping* and *dehumanizing* each other. If we frame the conflict as a competition over scarce resources, and truly believe that our survival as a group is dependent on overcoming the other side, we may quickly find ourselves generalizing about and stereotyping the other side, which often culminates in dehumanization, at which point acts of violence seem justified.

Throughout the conflict, Israelis and Palestinians have routinely viewed each other with suspicion and hatred, through the lenses of dehumanizing stereotypes and generalizations. This process has had tragic consequences, resulting in deaths on both sides. Once a group has been dehumanized, "behaviors that would be unacceptable or outrageous if directed toward those

---

7. Kelman, "Role of National Identity," 192.

'like oneself' are now permitted toward those who are 'so different'; [as] the moral insensitivity of one side triggers and justifies the same from the other."[8]

In most cases, intractable conflicts occur between two groups living in close proximity. It is much easier to stir up hatred and anger toward an enemy who is close by. It is easy to "show" that the enemy is stealing jobs, land, culture, or any other contested resource. This is why *proximity* is so often a factor in intractable conflicts, because it facilitates a cycle of violence and retaliation that would not be possible if the two sides lived farther away from one another. This dynamic also increases the likelihood of an escalation of violence, since each violent act is a reaction to violence itself.

Proximity has been a major factor in the Israeli-Palestinian conflict, where "the enemy" lives only a few kilometers away, and in some cases, just a few streets away, or even next door. Violence tends to beget violence, making peace negotiations difficult and making any ceasefire or treaty signed very fragile and easy to ignore or break. We see what theorists have called "reciprocal causation" at work, "where the response mechanism within the cycle of violence and counter violence becomes the cause for perpetuating the conflict, especially where groups have experienced mutual animosity for decades, if not generations."[9]

Every conflict, but especially intractable conflict, sees the development of *historical narratives* and *sacred truths* on both sides. This is part of a natural development that occurs among all groups, since the collective experience as a group is part of what binds it together. The problem is that, in conflict situations, and specifically in intractable conflicts, both sides have conflicting historical narratives which are essential to their identity and to the legitimacy of their cause. The ways in which we understand and frame our past says a lot about our self-perception and self-image as a group. In conflict, both sides usually portray themselves as the innocent victim and the other side as the aggressor. The narrative we tell ourselves becomes sacred, almost myth-like in its significance to our legitimacy. Any attempt to question or challenge it can be painful and usually encounters stiff resistance. The phenomenon of competing historical narratives can become a very real obstacle to reconciliation in intractable conflicts because, usually, the longer the conflict continues, the further entrenched the historical narrative becomes.

It is difficult to overemphasize the importance of the issue of conflicting historical narratives in the context of the Israeli-Palestinian struggle. It is

---

8. Augsburger, *Conflict Mediation across Cultures*, 51.
9. Lederach, *Building Peace*, 15.

impossible to imagine a form of Israeli identity and legitimacy that ignores the Holocaust, just as imagining Palestinian identity without the *Nakba*[10] is unthinkable. For both sides, portraying themselves as the sole victim is linked to the way the violence committed against the other is justified. An individual's personal experience is ignored, especially if it includes a positive interaction with the other, because that does not reinforce the group historical narrative, which takes precedence. In the Israeli-Palestinian context we see this clearly; Israelis say, "We were kicked out by the Romans," and Palestinians say, "We were kicked out in 1948." In the Israeli-Palestinian conflict, each side views itself as the native or indigenous people and the other side as the invader.

The Israeli-Palestinian conflict is a very good example of an intractable conflict, centered as it is on territory contested by two national movements, the Palestinian national movement and the Jewish national movement (Zionism). It exhibits many of the characteristics of an intractable conflict, in that it is protracted; violent; focused on fundamental goals; has been widely considered a zero-sum, irreconcilable conflict; and involves conflicting worldviews and identities.

Conflict Transformation

Conflict transformation has made a significant impact on the discipline of peace and conflict studies, leading theorists to reevaluate the generally assumed negative nature of conflict. Conflict is the product of energy, and it also generates a lot of energy, which may be harnessed, channeled, and directed constructively.

Conflict transformation differs from conflict resolution or conflict management in that it seeks not merely to contain or resolve the conflict but to radically transform it. The goal is not a political settlement, where both sides are satisfied with the outcome, but the loftier goal of reconciliation, which is the "redefinition and restoration of broken relationships."[11] For this sort of transformation to occur, we must change our outlook. A good start is to accept that conflict is inevitable and to endeavor to see its potential benefits.

We know that wherever there is human interaction there is conflict and that *conflicts are usually signals that there is a problem that needs to be taken care of.* When two children are fighting, it is usually because one provoked the

---

10. *Nakba* is a term commonly used by Palestinians to refer to the 1947–48 war, which for them was a "catastrophe," which is the literal meaning of the Arabic word.

11. Lederach, *Building Peace*, 75.

other, and action must be taken to restore the relationship. Children usually fight as the result of an injustice or a misunderstanding, and the same causes are usually at the root of more serious conflicts. However, simply managing the conflict and suppressing the root causes will not lead to a lasting, sustainable solution.[12]

If we focus our attention on the root causes of conflict and direct our energy toward addressing them, we can begin to *transform the conflict*. Rather than expend energy "proving" we are right, and further entrenching ourselves in our positions, we can channel that energy toward restoring broken relationships. Instead of a cycle of anger and violence, we can create a cycle of peace and development, but only if we confront conflict head on, for peace is "a consequence of confronting and overcoming conflict, not avoiding it."[13]

---

12. Reychler and Paffenholz, *Peacebuilding*, 3.
13. Arnold, *Seeking Peace*, 21.

5

The Voice of Vision

By Salim J. Munayer

The voice of John the Baptist crying out in the wilderness echoes and resonates in our lives today. He was crying out for repentance and for a change in people's lives. This call still needs to be heeded.

People are losing hope that the Israeli-Palestinian conflict will ever be resolved. Many have become apathetic or fatalistic, seeing no solution to the pain, hatred, and violence that has become such a regular part of daily life for both peoples. Our vision may be distorted as we begin to think that there is nothing beyond the conflict, which we view from only one side. Wearing these cultural/national blinders, our perspective is so limited that truth may easily be obscured. This is when we most need to heed John's call.

Even in John the Baptist's time, his call must have seemed strange. After all, Jerusalem was the core of Jewish social and spiritual life, with the temple at its epicenter. It was the most natural place where people met God, praised him, and felt his presence. But John was led to leave Jerusalem, to leave the temple, and go into the wilderness to find God. This was a radical departure. His role was to prepare the way for the Messiah, but it was also to shake people out of their cynical complacency and daily routine and to grant them a new perspective. Removing oneself to the wilderness, or the desert, was an essential part of this message, which today is more important than ever. We must return to the fundamentals. We have placed our trust in material possessions and forgotten that God is in control, and he is the one we should trust. We must remember our days in the wilderness and how we would have perished had God not provided us with manna. We would have been lost had God not led us with a cloud of smoke by day and a pillar of fire by night. We must focus on building relationships and remember that God is bigger than our conflict. He is the only one who can stop it, and he commands us to reach out in love and seek peace with our brothers and sisters.

There is also a problem of vision. For too long we have trusted political and financial institutions to deal exclusively with problems. In leaving everything up to them, we the community of God, the body of the Messiah, have become passive and have lost our vision. American writer and political activist Jim Wallis claims that when it comes to vision, our political and financial leaders are in danger of falling into one of two traps. The first is to have no vision at all, and the second is to have the wrong vision. These he describes as "visions that defend wealth and power, rather than opening up more opportunity; that are more exclusionary than inclusive . . . that exalt private interests over the common good; that simply leave too many people behind; that seek national or corporate self-interest over international peace and justice, or that increase conflict rather than reducing it."[1]

But there is good news! Both the lack of vision and the wrong vision are easily overcome because God has made the true vision available for us if we chose to seek it. We must pray for our political leaders, but we must not allow them to charge forward visionless or with the wrong vision. There is a voice crying out in the wilderness of violence, hatred, corruption, and scandal. It is calling us to return to God's vision, where "slaveries are ended, civil rights achieved, freedom established, compassion implemented, justice advanced, human rights defended, and peace made."[2]

---

1. Wallis, *God's Politics*, 29.
2. Wallis, 28.

6

The Transformative Power of Conflict

By Joshua Korn

For most people, the word "conflict" has negative connotations, as it is commonly associated with images and emotions related to anger, violence, war, and death. Often the word conjures thoughts or memories of trauma we have experienced personally, violent acts we have witnessed or participated in, or disagreements at home or with friends. We have all experienced some level of conflict, and understandably tend to instinctively shy away from it. However, conflict is a natural phenomenon, observable wherever there is interaction between people. It is unavoidable and must be addressed.

The idea of seeing positive potential in conflict is not new. It stretches back to the beginning of Western thought and the ancient Ionian philosopher Heraclitus, who viewed life as existing in a state of constant flux and observed that without conflict no progress was possible. His dialectical paradigm led him to state, "It should be understood that war is the common condition . . . and that all things come to pass through the compulsion of strife."[1] He even claimed that more than a necessary evil, conflict is an absolute requirement: "Homer was wrong in saying 'Would that strife might perish from amongst gods and men.' For if that were to occur, then all things would cease to exist."[2]

This recognition of the inevitability and positive potential of conflict in human affairs and in all of existence is a common theme among many great philosophers. Hegel's dialectic is probably the most well-known example, for

---

1. Heraclitus, *Complete Fragments*.
2. Heraclitus.

he claimed that God (or the Absolute) and history work together and employ conflict on spiritual and political levels to bring about change and arrive at idealized perfection. Marx's theory of historical materialism works with the same dialectic dynamics on the social level and interprets class war as an inevitable conflict that should eventually lead to a classless utopian society. Even Darwin's theory of natural selection is based on the necessity for conflict in the form of competition, which ultimately contributes to the survival of a species.

The difference between these historical-intellectual models and what the advocates of conflict transformation are suggesting is that while an aspect of justice and reconciliation colors the latter, the former are largely influenced by a "might equals right" or "survival of the fittest" sentiment. However, both acknowledge the inevitability of conflict, with conflict transformation recognizing that "conflicts signal problems that need to be taken care of."[3] However, rather than merely making observations and attempting to predict its eventual outcome, it seeks to *transform* the conflict into a "spiral of peace and development instead of a spiral of violence and destruction."[4]

This is an important distinction, for often a settlement which resolves a conflict does not confront its root causes. Due to political considerations, the essence of a conflict is often not discussed. The unfortunate result of this, usually calculated, oversight is that there is great likelihood of a reemergence of the conflict, as is clear in the context of the Israeli-Arab conflict. For the first few decades of Israel's existence, Israel fought and made peace with neighboring Arab countries and had little or no dealings with the Palestinians. Ignoring one of the root causes of the conflict is one of the reasons that it has continued for so long. Without confronting the problems at the core of the conflict, we will achieve nothing: "We want peace, but we want it on our own terms. We want an easy peace. Yet peace cannot come quickly or easily if it is to have any genuine staying power."[5]

In late April 2008, I participated in a Musalaha Youth Desert Encounter between thirty Israeli and Palestinian youth in the Arava Desert in southern Israel. Our purpose was to provide a setting where friendships could develop beyond political or social borders and to facilitate frank and honest discussion with the goal of arriving at reconciliation. As future leaders, youth must be involved in the process of reconciliation if the conflict is to be transformed.

---

3. Reychler and Paffenholz, *Peacebuilding*, 3.
4. Lederach, *Building Peace*, 84–85.
5. Arnold, *Seeking Peace*, 21.

In one activity, we divided participants into two groups and asked them for a list of words or images that define the Israeli-Palestinian conflict for them. The resulting words included: injustice, blood, discrimination, wall, security (or lack thereof), soldiers, and flags. The discussion became quite heated. For example, one Israeli inquired about the wall which separates the West Bank from Israel, asking if it was really such a problem and whether it actually interferes in the lives of those who live nearby. From the Israeli side, she said, it hardly interfered at all and was barely visible. Her comment was sincere in that, having never been there, she truly did not know what it was like on the Palestinian side, but it angered some of the Palestinian youth who were quick to point out to her just how intrusive this wall is in their lives.

Asked how he feels when he sees soldiers, a Palestinian responded that he feels excited at the prospect of throwing rocks at them. He claimed that this action was justified since soldiers come only to hurt or kill Palestinians. An argument ensued when another participant said that soldiers do not always kill Palestinians and that it is wrong to assume that they do. Israelis spoke of their friends or relatives in the army and became very defensive. The discussions were dominated by a few vocal participants on both sides, while most people remained silent. However, later on, many participants wanted to talk about the issues in a more intimate setting.

Although often difficult and upsetting, these discussions are essential to the reconciliation process. We have to be able to listen to one another, even when it makes us uncomfortable. "True peace is not merely a lofty cause that can be taken up and pursued with good intentions. Nor is it something to be simply had or bought. Peace demands struggle."[6] Although the temptation is strong to avoid discussion of the divisive issues, especially among believers who can always fall back on their common faith in the Messiah, we cannot dodge this stage of the reconciliation process if we truly want peace. For peace is "a consequence of confronting and overcoming conflict, not avoiding it."[7]

In Philippians 4:6–9, we are promised the "peace of God, which transcends all understanding" (v. 7). It is easy to see how this peace can apply to our spiritual lives because of the inner peace we have in the knowledge of God's forgiveness and redemption of our sins. However, this peace is holistic and encompasses far more than a spiritual, internal peace. It also implies a practical, tangible peace that has concrete applications in the work of reconciliation. Notice how we are told we can attain this peace by "prayer and petition" (v.

---

6. Arnold, 21.
7. Arnold, 21.

6) but also by meditating on "whatever is true, whatever is noble, whatever is right, whatever is pure, whatever is lovely, whatever is admirable" (v. 8). This is very practical advice, exhorting us to be on the side of justice and truth and to seek them out in all situations.

Not only are we meant to meditate on these things, but in verse 9 we are told, "Whatever you have learned or received or heard from me, or seen in me – put it into practice. And the God of peace will be with you." It is important to remember that we are being asked to take action. Note the words used: "put it into practice" (v. 9). We are commanded to perform these virtues in our lives, which translates into seeking peace and transforming our conflicts. Some might argue that the noble thing is to politely avoid conflict, but if our goal is to achieve real, lasting peace and reconciliation, we must tell the truth in love and face the problems causing our conflict. This is our noble, lovely, just, and true task, and if we take it up, God's peace will be our reward.

7

Listening

From Musalaha's *A Curriculum of Reconciliation*

Learning to listen is an essential skill for people in conflict. On a daily basis, both Israelis and Palestinians talk at and past each other, repeatedly failing to communicate. This section provides guidelines for becoming an effective listener.

Listening: Tell Me Again, I Want to Hear You

Listening and the need to be listened to are integral parts of our lives which both form and influence our identities. Professor and counselor David Augsburger says, "Being heard is so close to being loved that for the average person they are almost indistinguishable."[1] To have effective communication, we must be open to *hearing each other*. Each person is unique and distinct, yet we often expect from others what we expect from ourselves. When emotions are heated, we often cease to *hear the differences* between ourselves and those with whom we are communicating. It is a sign of maturity when we can recognize and appreciate the uniqueness of others and not expect them to behave as we do.

At the same time, it is important to understand and *hear our similarities*. Whether we are quiet and someone else is loud, or we are adventurous and someone else is more cautious, we all have similar needs, desires, and dreams. We "need not reject any person as beyond understanding."[2] Augsburger notes some of what we share as humans: "We cannot live without hope. We become a self through will. We venture into life with purpose. We strive for some

---

1. Augsburger, *Caring Enough*, 12.
2. Augsburger, 18.

competence. We search for identity. We long for love. We learn to care. We discover wisdom."[3]

Most often, conflict between people arises from their similarities, not their differences. What we share may also be a source of frustration. To truly listen to one another we must *hear all of each other* – the happiness and the sadness, the contentment and also the bitterness. All humans need to be heard fully and a listener can choose to hear the complexity, paradoxes, and richness of the whole person.

Usually, when we listen, the other's words are filtered through our expectations, experiences, and interpretations, so that we often hear only what we want to hear or what we supposedly fear to have confirmed. Part of being an attentive listener is being self-aware, *hearing oneself and hearing the other*. If we are aware of our fears or expectations concerning the person speaking, we can better separate our own perceptions from what is actually being said. For example, our Jewish/Israeli/Arab/Palestinian worldviews act as filters for how we interpret what we hear.

Augsburger provides a list to keep in mind when thinking about the meaning being communicated by another person. He writes that: "Meanings are in persons, not in words, words don't mean, people mean; they are not [only] transmitted in oral communication, [but also with] oral and visual signals – sounds, words, pauses, tones, omissions, facial expressions, gesture, posture; and they are interpreted based on inferences and hunches, not on facts. Just as the wrapper is not the chocolate, the word is not the meaning. Communication is a meeting of meanings and one person's meanings will never perfectly match another's."[4]

Augsburger further notes, "In good communication the intent equals the impact."[5] Good communication takes place when the speaker's intended meaning filters through the speaker's perceptions, passes through the listener's perceptions, and is understood by the listener as the speaker intended.

Therefore, the speaker and the listener both share responsibility for speaking and understanding correctly, taking into account that both are influenced by their perceptions. The speaker must try to take into consideration how the listener will hear what is said, and the listener must try to set aside any perceptions she has that may prevent her from hearing as intended. While

---

3. Augsburger.
4. Augsburger, 25–26.
5. Augsburger, 26.

understanding perfectly is impossible, it is still a goal we strive toward in communication.[6]

Attending: Try Me Again, I'm Listening

Whenever we experience strong feelings, whether positive or negative, we are unable to truly hear the other person. However, there are a number of steps we can take toward hearing openly.

The first step to hearing another is *to be present*. The next step is to really *pay attention* to what is being communicated, both verbally and nonverbally. Step three is to take *authentic interest* in the communicator's views and perceptions, regardless of our agreement with the speaker. In step four, one *suspends judgment* or pushes aside perceptions and opinions in order to be open to what is being communicated. The next step is *patience*, and refraining from interrupting, while the sixth and final suggestion is to be *committed to work* toward the goal of successful communication, successful listening, and then successful dialogue based on the equal sharing of views and opinions.

In our daily lives we are assailed by advertisements and messages from media and other sources, and we learn to be *selective* about the messages we choose to process. We do the same with the people with whom we interact. Our selectivity filters the information we encounter, so that we tend to remember best those things that we liked or disliked the most and not what we deemed unimportant. For example, shortly after an argument with a close friend or spouse, if you discuss what happened and what was said, two different versions often emerge. We remember the things that pleased or offended us the most, and these differ for different people. Since we can't process every message, selectivity is both an asset and a liability. We listen selectively and may not attend to important messages which can contribute to fuller understanding.

In our selectivity, we often *rule out speakers*. For example, "I do not listen to . . ." (Muslims, Orthodox Jews, the Israeli army, the Palestinian news, the Israeli news, etc.). Sometimes we rule out speakers who are close to us, such as a nagging child, a friend who always complains, or an annoying co-worker. We rule out those who we imagine don't have anything important to say, but we are offended if we are treated in that way. We can choose not to rule out others who are trying to communicate with us. We can choose to listen to someone despite what they may have said or done in the past.

---

6. Augsburger, 32.

Another obstacle to true communication and true listening is the tendency to *reach premature conclusions*. Sometimes, assuming we know what a person is going to say, we tune out the words, cheating both sides of the communication. We should strive to put aside our premature conclusions, or prejudices, and listen with full attention.

Another obstacle to listening is *reading in motivations*. Sometimes we assume something about the communicator, and as a result, we may be oversensitive and quick to hear rejection or dismissiveness. Augsburger writes, "When [we] have a hunch about the other's motives, [we] will tend to hear it confirmed in everything said."[7] We have to work against the tendency to project what we believe the speaker's motives to be, as this prevents us from truly listening.

Sometimes when listening to a speaker we can *read in threats* where there are none. As a result of hearing a threat, we often stop the speaker or stop listening. But by continuing to listen to the speaker, we might find that in fact a threat was not expressed. Alternatively, if there was something threatening in the speaker's words, by hearing them out, we can respond intelligently, instead of replying in anger or frustration.

We generally think four times as fast as we speak. This means we understand a speaker's words faster than he or she can say them, so we may *let our minds wander* instead of fully listening. To be effective listeners, we must choose to listen and keep our minds focused.

When someone is speaking and we wish to add something or to disagree, we sometimes *rehearse a response* in our minds, so we won't forget it, and search for a break in conversation. This is always at the expense of listening, and we may miss important elements of what the speaker is saying that could correct our assumptions or even make our response unnecessary.

Sometimes we *react to trigger words* and stop listening. For example, if a speaker uses a term we find racist, sexist, or patronizing, we may have an emotional response to the word which prevents us from hearing the entirety of what is being said. To prevent this, we must identify those trigger words for ourselves and discuss them with the speaker if possible – and also come to terms with the vocabulary we find offensive so it will not be an obstacle to listening.

When we listen to someone, we tend to *respond with evaluation* before understanding what was said. When we listen, we generally evaluate, interpret, support, probe, and then (finally) understand. Evaluation includes distancing

---

7. Augsburger, 48.

oneself from the speaker and passing judgment. One can evaluate by saying that what someone said was smart, funny, or unclear, or by stating that one does not appreciate the speaker's attitude. If we know that evaluation prevents true listening, we can train ourselves to listen to *understand* what is being said prior to *evaluating* it.

Sometimes when we dislike the person who is speaking, we refuse to listen. When we face someone with a very different personality, we may *reject the person or personality*, and at times, it is those who are most similar to us whom we find irritating.

When we refuse to listen for the above reasons, we mistake a person's method of communication (which is filtered through his or her personality) for the entire message that is being conveyed. We must look past the things that prevent us from hearing others and learn to value people regardless of their personality or our affinity for them – "Listening is the most elemental language for such valuing."[8]

Hearing: I Want to Hear; I Want to Be Heard

A good relationship is dependent on good and equal communication which allows for dialogue. There are various levels of communication. In order from lowest to highest, there is *threat, manipulation, bargaining, persuasion*, and finally, *dialogue*. No relationship is required in order to threaten someone; a little bit of knowledge about someone is required to manipulate them; a closer relationship is necessary to bargain with them; and a deeper one is necessary for persuasion. The highest level of communication is dialogue, in which two sides share and discuss issues of mutual importance. In true dialogue, equal communication enables both sides to feel they have been equally heard and appreciated. It takes time for relationships to reach the level of dialogue, but once they are firmly established it is easy to open a conversation directly on that level – although, during periods of stress, dialogue can revert to being more difficult to achieve.

Principles which contribute to equal communication include equal hearing, equal ownership, equal presence, equal integrity, equal responsibility, equal conciliation, and equal freedom.

---

8. Augsburger, 54.

Leveling: I Want Equality; I Will Hear You Equally

When we communicate, we often speak either vertically or horizontally. In speaking vertically, we either "talk up" or "talk down" to others. We talk down when we blame, scold, judge, belittle, instruct, supervise, etc. We talk up when we placate, apologize, grovel, ingratiate, or yield. We often excel at one or the other but have difficulty *leveling*, or speaking horizontally – conversing as equals who both listen to and hear one another. A number of steps can help us to speak to one another horizontally.

Step one is to *suspend judgment*. We often encounter people whose opinions and values are unlike our own and we must learn to suspend judgment so as to hear them with sincere respect and concern, without our own strongly held views interfering. Despite adhering to different definitions or versions of reality, we can still listen openly. One approach is to use "bracketing." Augsburger describes this technique as follows:

> [Although I thoroughly disagree with what you just said,] I will listen to hear how you arrived at your point of view and to discover what is so attractive to you in that way of thinking. [If I bracket my judgment,] I will not lose my concern, nor will I use it to filter yours.[9]

As we see, bracketing allows us to hear the other person while placing our opinions "on hold." It allows us to more fully understand the other without our opinions getting in the way. By bracketing, we respect the other. Also, to suspend judgment we must bracket our tendency to label others. We are not the sum of our political, ideological, or theological opinions – a nationalist, Communist, pacifist, humanist, dispensationalist, etc. We are more than the various aspects of our opinions. As humans, we are free to change, correct, abandon, or strengthen our opinions. If we can bracket the point of view a speaker is expressing at any moment, we can respect and accept someone even while disagreeing with their views. We should be able to confront a view as a wrong view without seeing a person as a "wrong" person. We must learn to express our differences and disagreements without belittling the speaker.

The next step in leveling is for both speaker and listener to *disconnect self-esteem*. Our self-esteem is often connected to the other's reactions to what we say. If the other person is not listening or is disapproving, we may fear we are boring or that our words lack value. However, to speak horizontally we must disconnect from the tendency to link our self-esteem to the other's response

---

9. Augsburger, 102.

or reaction, for in doing so we are more concerned about someone's opinion of us than with communicating.

As children, when we perform well, we are often praised by our parents, who hope that this will motivate us to continue to behave in a certain way. However, linking self-esteem with performance is problematic, for our worth is not determined by our performance but is intrinsic to us as people. We are thinkers, agents, and doers, not thoughts, decisions, or deeds. And we may change our thoughts and decisions and deeds. We must learn not to view a person's disagreement as rejection or critique of our very being.

The third step in leveling is to *define yourself*. When we speak, we should take responsibility for what we are feeling. For example, note the difference between the statements below:

> We should be much more cooperative so things wouldn't get so tense around here; you get the feeling that no one wants to cooperate with anybody else around here; they say that [our] productivity is directly related to [our] ability to work cooperatively.
>
> It's a real source of frustration to everyone when cooperation is as low as it has been recently; I'm not happy with the level of cooperation [here]; I'm willing to put in some extra time to work on it with [you].[10]

In the above statements, the latter "I" statement is the most honest and responsible. When we take an "I" position, we are responders, not reactors; free agents, not victims of a situation. "I" statements are empowering and do not allow a situation to oppress us. We cannot speak for anyone else. "I" statements are the most honest, for we can only measure "how I see it, how I evaluate it, what I want to do now."[11] By using "I" language we reduce the possibilities of blaming or manipulating someone else, and speak to each other as equals. We must allow others to define their own positions, and we must define ours.

The fourth step to leveling is learning to *discard questions*. When abused, questions can be used to manipulate, shame, blame, criticize, or trap a person. To communicate on the same level, we should make statements. For example, instead of saying, "Isn't it true that . . . ." – which is a leading question – we should say, "I believe that. . . ." Or instead of saying, "When are you going to . . . ," say, "I want change."[12] We should use questions to gather information but not to replace statements.

---

10. Augsburger, 106–107.
11. Augsburger, 109.
12. Augsburger, 113.

The final step to leveling is to *reply simply*. When listening, it is important to demonstrate your attention by inviting the speaker to continue so as to explore more deeply what he or she is saying. *Repeating* a key word from a speaker's statement conveys interest and attention. We can also *reflect* on a certain statement or feeling expressed by rephrasing it, and we can *request* further information. Another way to express interest is via statements of *understanding* and *support* when a speaker shares a deep feeling or vulnerable information. Finally, we can offer an *interpretation* to suggest a different perspective.

When leveling, or speaking horizontally, our verbal responses are only part of the message. Tone may comprise up to 38 percent of emotional impact, while body language may constitute up to 58 percent. It is important to maintain the tone and body language conducive to true dialogue.

Risking: I Want to Know You; I Want to Be Known

For a relationship to develop, there must be trust and the ability to take risks. We all have two poles of self-disclosure: (1) fearing that if people knew what we were truly like, they would not love us, while (2) believing that if people only understood us, then they would love us. The former causes us to push people away, while the latter encourages us to seek people out. These two poles are in a constant tug of war. If the former wins, we tend to reveal too little about ourselves, while if the latter side prevails the result is the reverse.

The reticent person is usually more cautious and controlled, while the more open type tends to be warm and garrulous, but possibly more demanding. To be effective communicators, we strive for a balance between respect for privacy and responsiveness to openness. In a healthy relationship, both (or all) involved decide together on the pace at which self-disclosure occurs.

Learning how open we can be and with whom is part of our maturing experience as we age, and our self-disclosure and interaction with others allow us to know ourselves better. While privacy is important and a privilege, it is not a value or end in itself, and some of our deepest needs may be met through positive interaction with others.

Caring: I Will Value You as I Want to Be Valued

When people are suffering through difficult situations, the best way to care is often to simply listen rather than give advice. This can provide "the gift of presence" which often proves more comforting than words.[13] However,

---

13. Augsburger, 149.

not all listening demonstrates caring. One may listen to gather data or listen with sympathy; one may listen in order to gossip, listen inquisitively, or listen helpfully by offering verbal support. Caring can be manifested in numerous ways.

1. When we care about people, we encourage them to grow and be the best versions of themselves they can be.

2. When caring includes listening it has even more potential to heal, and when a listener reflects what someone has to say, they may provide the speaker with enhanced clarity. This may not cure the pain, but the point is not to cure the speaker but rather to care for them. The caring listener seeks to hear the pain without trivializing it, and this attention makes way for the healing that can come from within the speaker. Healing may begin as the speaker sorts through thoughts and feelings and the listener provides moral and verbal support. The listener should be attentive to the feelings of worth and hope beneath the despair of depression and may gently remind the speaker of their worth.

3. When our need to be acknowledged as beings of worth is threatened, we may react with anger. When listening to someone who is angry, it is important to be attuned to what is expressed. As listeners, we can reaffirm the speaker's worth and help them to deal responsibly with their anger. A careful listener can help the speaker confront anger without passing judgment.

4. Although resentment is usually a self-defeating cycle, a caring listener should have the patience to help the speaker come to terms with it. We cannot change the past, but we can make changes in the present that will affect our future attitudes.

5. Augsburger writes, "In listening we become truly *with* another. In caring we become truly *for* another."[14] Together, these are at the core of a positive and healthy relationship. Caring and listening grant us heightened awareness of who we are and of the person we are listening to and also contribute to a deeper relationship.[15]

---

14. Augsburger, 166.
15. This list is adapted from Augsburger, 166–169.

8

Women's Narrative: The Art of Listening

By Louise Thomsen

The historical narrative is the storyteller's reflection of the reality of their historical past. Other historical narratives may include the same events, seen from a different perspective. In areas of conflict, a narrative usually tells the story of how the conflict was caused by the other side, how "our" actions are justified as self-defense, and how the other side continues to violate our basic rights.

Since the narrative paints its own people as heroic victims fighting evil, it is a powerful tool to motivate the people and the international community to fight on one side's behalf. It is constantly repeated in schools, the media, and conversations and becomes imprinted in people's minds to such an extent that it is perceived as historical truth and often mistaken for history. Although a historical narrative contains historical facts, it provides a subjective, selective, one-sided perspective of the truth.

This was apparent at our women's conference in Cyprus. The forty women were divided into two groups, one Israeli and one Palestinian. We asked the Israelis to present the Palestinian narrative and the Palestinians to present the Israeli story. Both groups struggled to detach themselves from their own narrative as they tried to tell the story from the other's perspective. Some cried, "We can't say that; it is not the truth," while others countered, "It may not be our truth, but it is their truth, and we have been asked to present their truth, whether we agree with it or not."

Many of the women realized that their knowledge of the other's narrative and history was very limited, and that in knowing only their own narrative, they have but a partial picture of the truth about the history of their people and the conflict. In their search for truth, they were challenged to check the historical accuracy of their own narrative, which might result in having to modify it. Changing your own truth is a difficult challenge and, for some, a shocking realization.

Listening to the two historical narratives, it struck me that they are a hindrance to reconciliation because they are based on two very different foundations. This difference results in misunderstandings because Israelis and Palestinians are speaking from different perspectives and are thus having two different conversations.

The Israeli narrative is primarily based on theological interpretations of the Torah and the Bible, which are often repeated by religious Jews, secular Jews, and Messianic Jews when discussing the conflict. In reconciliation and peace efforts, participants require common ground to unite them and foster commitment to the reconciliation process. Among believers, the factor that unites us is our faith in Jesus Christ as our savior. This is why we sometimes call the first stage in the reconciliation process the "hallelujah stage." We come together as Israelis and Palestinians because we are brothers and sisters and we believe that God commanded us to love each other and to seek peace together. Our faith is also our comfort zone which reunites us when other issues threaten to divide us.

However, it seems to me that when we talk historical narrative, our faith threatens to become a stumbling block because different interpretations of the Bible lead us to exclude rather than include one another. I often hear believers on both sides saying that we should not deal with issues related to the conflict; our only focus should be our faith, and we will be reconciled. But when we have different theological interpretations, we are not able to reconcile without working through them and reaching a theology of reconciliation.

As humans, we cannot detach ourselves from the conflict around us, as we are caught up in the narrative of our own people and in the theological interpretations – the power play and the feelings of anger, pain, blame and guilt. These do not disappear because we are believers, but affect our behavior, actions, and reactions. I see this every time believers meet, and we saw it again at the conference as each side claimed ownership of the whole truth. Blame quickly became the focal point. As one participant said, "It is important to discuss the issues that relate to the conflict because it builds a foundation that won't shake when something happens."

The Palestinian narrative is based on a victim mentality and the search for justice. The Palestinian people have suffered, and continue to suffer, great pain and loss throughout the Israeli-Palestinian conflict. As one Israeli participant said, "The Palestinian suffering is greater and more acute than the Israeli suffering." But there are victims on both sides of a conflict and the pain of both sides must be recognized. Remaining in a victim mindset is paralyzing and provokes a need to blame someone for the pain. It also prevents you from listening to the sufferings of the other.

During our discussions, almost all the women expressed pain and suffering in their lives caused by the conflict. We often hear the words blame, guilt, apology, repentance, and forgiveness, and maybe we have become too focused on these concepts. As we listened to the personal testimonies of hardship, the women started asking each other, "What do you need from me to lessen your pain?" When we asked this question, which we should have asked long ago, not one woman said that she needed an apology or for someone to admit guilt and request forgiveness.

The women asked each other to simply listen. Listen to my pain, my suffering, my truth, my narrative. And accept it as my pain, my suffering, my truth, and my narrative. You do not have to agree with it but accept it as mine. One woman used the metaphor of having a headache. It is not very helpful when every time you tell someone that you have a headache, the answer is, "So do I." Sometimes you just want someone to say, "That's awful. I am so sorry that you are not feeling well. I hope that you will feel better soon." You just want compassion. We are so caught up in our zero-sum mentality of win-lose and blaming each other for our sufferings that we forget to show compassion. This weekend the women committed themselves to listen to each other's story. Not to argue or agree, but to listen and respect.

Stage Two

Opening Up

9

Identity in Conflict and Reconciliation

From Musalaha's *A Curriculum of Reconciliation*

The term *identity* describes how a person sees himself/herself as a separate and unique individual. As we grow from childhood to adulthood, our concept of identity develops in stages as a result of our self-reflection and interaction with others. Our social setting, authority figures, peers, religious leaders, and teachers all help shape our identities. Recognition and acknowledgement or their absence from any of the above can contribute to a positive or negative identity.

We develop identities as individuals and as part of social groups. Our social identities (or group identities) are formed in reaction to and in interaction with other groups. As a result, there is no "pure," single identity. Our interaction with other groups shapes and forms our identities, and consequently, the group or people we define ourselves as different from become part of our identity.

To some degree, identity is a matter of choice, but for the most part it is influenced by our experiences and personal history.[1] Various fields of study analyze the concept differently and focus on the personal or social aspects separately or together. Psychologists, anthropologists, philosophers, sociologists, and political scientists all study different aspects of identity and how individuals relate to themselves, the social context, others, etc. This section explores some of the elements which comprise the personal and social aspects of identity and considers its importance.

---

1. Volf, *Exclusion and Embrace*, 19.

What Is Identity?

Identity has only been considered a subject worthy of academic study for the past fifty to sixty years, in the wake of postmodernism and multiculturalism,[2] and scholars in various fields focus on different aspects.

If you ask yourself, "Who am I?" the words which immediately spring to mind reveal your concept of identity and the parts of your identity you consider to be most important. Identity has been defined as how one defines oneself; how one defines oneself in relation to others; how individuals and groups define themselves, and are defined by others, based on race, ethnicity, language, and culture; and the relationship of the other to oneself.[3] A further definition: identity is comprised of social categories and is the source of an individual's self-esteem.[4]

Part of identity development is distinguishing between oneself and others. One's identity is comprised of numerous categories, including the personal and social distinctions which characterize individuals and groups.

Identity requires awareness, and identity formation is active. It is not simply your personality, whether you are bubbly and outgoing or reserved and shy. We are all born into certain groups, and to some extent our identity is absorbed from and formed by our culture and those around us. There is always a matter of choice involved in identity. People may choose to assume a particular identity by converting to a certain religion, joining a community, or supporting a specific sports team. But sometimes identities are also thrust upon us. If you are part of a minority group, you may be treated poorly by the majority group and as a result develop certain defensive attitudes and behaviors. If you move from one place to another involuntarily as a refugee, or come from a family of refugees, this shapes your identity as well.[5]

When we meet new people, we often seek similarities, asking, "Where are you from? What do you do?" The answers to these questions may reveal whether we have anything in common or share some aspects of our identities, and when we do, we often feel a sense of shared belonging and familiarity with the other person. We may identify people as similar to us based on language, clothing, the way they look, or other external characteristics. If you have ever been in a foreign country where you do not understand the native language

---

2. Fearon, "What Is Identity?," 10, 36.
3. Hopf cited in Fearon, 11; Hogg and Abrams cited in Fearon, 2; Deng cited in Fearon, 1; Hall cited in Fearon, 5.
4. Fearon, 13, 24.
5. Open University, "What Is Identity."

and suddenly hear your mother tongue being spoken, you may feel close to the strangers who share that part of their identity with you.[6]

What Are the Main Components of Identity?
Social Identity

Identity has two main aspects: the social and the personal. To some extent, identity "is just a social category, a group of people designated by a label (or labels) that is commonly used either by the people designated, others, or both."[7] People adjust their attitudes, actions, and thoughts to suit their *social categories*, which provide them with a sense of belonging. A social category may be Palestinian, Israeli, mother, son, construction worker, or production assistant. One's social identity or category changes according to one's context. For example, if someone asks you who or what you are, your answer will be different based on the setting and who is asking. You might answer "I'm Palestinian," or "I'm a mother," or "I'm a driver," or "I'm a communist," depending on the context. Identity as a social category is defined by rules of membership and is understood by characteristics or content.[8]

Social categories usually comprise role or type identities. Some examples of roles are father, prime minister, or student. Some examples of types are sexual identity, ethnic identity, or categories related to political affiliation.[9]

Our social categories dictate some of our behaviors, as we view any group that we belong to as the "in-group," while all others are "out-groups." Our social identity naturally causes us to favor the in-group over the out-group,[10] and simply belonging to an in-group often results in more favorable feelings toward those in the in-group than those in the out-group.[11] To some degree, our in-group gains legitimacy through delegitimizing the out-group.[12]

Due to our dependence on, and inclusion in, in-groups, part of our self-image derives from our participation in various social groups. We often assume that everyone who is part of our in-group is similar to us. Likewise, we believe that people in our in-group have generally positive characteristics, and

---

6. Open University.
7. Fearon, "What Is Identity?," 10.
8. Fearon, 13–14.
9. Fearon, 17.
10. Stephan and Stephan, *Intergroup Relations*, 91.
11. Stephan and Stephan, 92.
12. Kelman, "Role of National Identity," 192.

are unique and interesting individuals, while people in the out-groups have negative characteristics. Without sustained interaction with members of an out-group, members of an in-group often assume that all members of an out-group are the same, which leads to generalizing and stereotyping. As we get to know members of an out-group, we begin to see its members as individuals. Of course, not all stereotyping is negative. For example, a positive stereotype is that Middle Eastern culture is warm and hospitable.[13] However, stereotyping is negative when it becomes an obstacle to intergroup relations. It may lead to justifying unfounded prejudices against an out-group, unwillingness to reevaluate in-group attitudes and behavior toward an out-group/stereotyped group, and preventing people in an out-group/stereotyped group from participating in certain activities, fields of work, etc. Stereotyping can lead to "self-fulfilling prophecy behavior" in the out-group. For example, if you always accuse a group of behaving in a violent, uncivilized manner and treat it as if it does, its behavior may begin to reflect that stereotype. Stereotyping can lead to in-group ignorance and out-group suffering, resulting in a cycle of misunderstanding, anger, and in extreme cases, violence.

When competition between two different groups leads to conflict, group members often adopt a zero-sum mentality and assume that in order to "win" the other group must "lose." Competition with an out-group may lead to hostility toward it, while resulting in increased in-group unity, organization, self-esteem, and teamwork. In other words, intergroup competition leads to intragroup cooperation in which intragroup differences tend to be ignored. Interestingly, the in-group will often persist in its self-bias, even when it suffers for it. One example is white governments in apartheid South Africa, which persisted in their unjust system despite the burden of international sanctions. Intergroup behavior is also influenced by self-esteem, self-knowledge, worldview, power, and control.[14]

Personal Identity

While personal identity may be constructed around a group/social identity, this isn't always the case.[15] Personal identity is "that which distinguishes you as an individual from other *individuals*."[16] Like social identity, it is influenced by

---

13. Stephan and Stephan, *Intergroup Relations*, 90–96.
14. Stephan and Stephan, 92–94, 101.
15. Fearon, "What Is Identity," 14.
16. Fearon, 22. Emphasis original.

self-esteem, to the extent that self-esteem may be the foundation of personal identity and may inform one's dignity, honor, pride, or self-respect. If asked "Who are you?" you would probably identify yourself according to the social category/group which you consider the most significant and to which you are most committed. This category takes precedence over other aspects of your identity when you make choices which may contradict additional social categories you belong to. Personal identity may range from moral principles (the framework in which you determine what you should or should not do) to personal style (the way you choose to dress – similarly or differently from people around you).[17] Professor James D. Fearon provides the following definition:

> Personal identity is a set of attributes, beliefs, desires, or principles of action that a person thinks distinguish her in socially relevant ways and that (a) the person takes special pride in; (b) the person takes no special pride in, but which orient her behavior such that she would be at a loss about how to act and what to do without them; or (c) the person feels she could not change even if she wanted to.[18]

Social vs. Personal Identity

There is an inverse relationship between your personal and social identities, for when you focus on yourself as a unique individual you are not focusing on yourself as part of a group, and when you focus on yourself as part of a group, you are not focusing on yourself as a unique individual.[19] Two individuals from two very different groups may have a lot in common on an interpersonal level – a Palestinian and an Israeli might both like soccer, certain types of food and music, and may be studying the same subjects in school – however, divisive social differences can remain. This does not mean that they cannot be friends. They can be, and Musalaha's reconciliation model encourages these interpersonal relationships, but this is not reconciliation in and of itself. Reconciliation of our conflict must include intergroup reconciliation.

Culture, ethnicity, nation, religion, gender, and other identity sub-categories are all contained within those of social and personal identity. While these specifics are not explored in this general overview, it should be interesting

---

17. Fearon, 11, 21–24.
18. Fearon, 25.
19. Stephan and Stephan, *Intergroup Relations*, 90.

to reflect on those aspects of your culture, ethnicity, nationality, religion, and gender which contribute to your social or personal identities.

Why Is It Important?
Identity Related to Action

Our personal and social identities prompt us to behave in certain ways, so that our actions can often be attributed to the categories to which we belong. Your definition of action is often related to a certain social category: he refused to serve in the army because he is a pacifist; she was not comfortable singing the Israeli national anthem because she is Palestinian; he is wearing a *kipah* because he is Jewish.

The mental connection we make between actions and the social categories which influence them show that we expect people in different categories to adhere to certain *social norms*. We also sometimes categorize people according to their actions and understand these as *social habits* (which may be linked to stereotypes). For example, if you are in a restaurant and you hear a group of people speaking very loudly, you might think, "They are speaking loudly so they must be American." You may associate certain traits with characteristics you believe to be common to a particular group.[20]

Identity can explain why we do what we do. Among others, we follow social norms for the following reasons: because we believe it is the right thing to do (for example, you do not lie because you believe it is immoral); to earn the approval of specific social or personal categories (for example, you refrain from littering in your neighborhood so you won't offend your neighbors); to be rewarded – or because we know if we don't, we won't be rewarded (for example, if you do not show up at your job and work for a certain number of hours, you will not receive your salary); and sometimes, simply because we do not know what else to do (for example, you might attend church on a weekly basis not because you necessarily believe in Christianity, but because your parents went to church every Sunday morning).[21]

Identity Related to Preference

Being a member of a certain social category does not mean that you wish to abide by all its attendant social norms. Various aspects of our identity are

---

20. Fearon, "What Is Identity?," 26–28.
21. Reasons adapted from Fearon, "What Is Identity?," 28–29.

always contradicting or competing with each other. For example, a professor may not enjoy publishing articles but will be sure to do so to increase her salary, enhance her reputation, maintain her professional standards, or achieve tenure. The reasons this professor publishes reveal her *preferences*. Preferences play an important role in our choices, and often reflect parts of our identity. Strategy and choice are inseparable parts of the construction of our identity.[22]

Identity Challenged

Comprised of deeply-rooted and significant feelings, when challenged, identity is a powerful motivator. If someone casts aspersions on your ethnicity or culture, you are often deeply hurt and offended as the negative comments violate or threaten your identity, and thereby your sense of belonging, self-esteem, meaning, connectedness, and recognition. The negative statement is deemed hostile because it "undermine[s] a person's basis for thinking well of himself or herself."[23] Such situations often lead to ethnic conflict, for when one group threatens another's identity, strong emotional reactions result, sometimes leading to outbreaks of violence. Some scholars suggest that ethnic conflicts erupt "from the pursuit of a feeling of comparative self-worth."[24]

Identity may be challenged by a majority group's attitude to a minority group. When two different cultural groups come into contact, both groups change as a result of the experience. Minority groups often strive to maintain their culture while at the same time orienting themselves toward the dominant majority culture.

Four possible acculturation strategies include: assimilation, separation, integration, and/or marginalization. *Assimilation* occurs when members of a minority group surrender their minority cultural identity to the majority cultural identity. *Separation* is the opposite situation, when the minority wishes to avoid interaction with the majority group to maintain its identity at all costs. *Integration* entails retaining one's minority culture, while participating in the majority culture. *Marginalization* results when members of a minority group do not believe it is possible (or don't care) to maintain their minority cultural identity and also have limited interest in being part of the majority cultural identity. These four acculturation strategies may be imposed on a minority group by a majority group. For example, if a majority or dominant

---

22. Fearon, 30–31.
23. Fearon, 24.
24. Horowitz, 1985, cited in Fearon, 24n30.

group believes in separation and imposes it on a minority group, separation will result. For integration to occur, both the majority and minority groups must agree, since it cannot occur without the cooperation of both parties.[25]

It is important to understand why we react as we do when our identity is challenged or when acculturation strategies are implemented. It is helpful to identify the various causes and effects that have changed and shaped our identities, particularly in situations of conflict. Often, during Stages One or Two, Palestinian and Israeli participants feel that their identity is threatened by the other party. In our encounter groups, we bring together people of different ethnic and cultural backgrounds and encourage discussions related to the conflict. We find that when identity is challenged, a common response is to challenge the identity of the other by undermining the other's self-worth or belonging to a people or a land.

Conclusion

Our identities are complex and multi-faceted, and we all have multiple layers within the broader designations of social and personal identity. Self-reflection and self-awareness are crucial when we discuss this subject. To understand others, we must also understand ourselves (including our needs for belonging, self-esteem, self-affirmation, etc.), and we can never fully understand ourselves if we do not learn to understand others. We should strive to respect our differences, rather than see them as negative or threatening. We must seek to accept the other as he or she wishes to be seen.

In the context of the Israeli-Palestinian conflict, national identities are constantly in competition, and each side tends to exclude the other, viewing itself as the in-group. Much of our identity is based on exclusion rather than inclusion and shunning rather than embrace. But throughout the journey of reconciliation, identities develop and change as we learn more about ourselves and others, and how each of us might have played a role in excluding the other. As we develop and mature, our identities continue to change, often becoming more nuanced as we react to and interact with others and specific events. Reconciliation encounters may play a role in shaping identity, particularly if participants choose to remain involved in the process.

In the upcoming section titled "Reclaiming Identity," we discuss how identity can move from exclusivity to inclusivity and even into embrace of the other.

---

25. Berry, "Immigration, Acculturation and Adaptation," 46, cited in Munayer, "Ethnic Identity," 49–50, adapted from David W. Augsburger, *Conflict Mediation across Cultures*, 16–18.

10

Mixing Oil and Water: A Messianic Jewish Perspective

By a Musalaha participant

I love the expression of wonder on a child's face when she encounters something for the first time. One of my favorite recollections of wonder as a child was when I saw oil poured into water. I tried to stir the solution faster and faster to see if the oil would dissolve, yet the little bubbles always pushed through the water to re-emerge in their previous state, as a layer of oil.

The same is often true of Jews and Arabs, and even Messianic Jews and Palestinian Christians. We don't mix. I am not saying that we don't attend each other's congregations or pray together at conferences. But we don't let our guard down, talk about the tough questions, or bring each other into our lives.

In these days of terrorism and occupation, it is not surprising that many, if not most, yield to the rhetoric of the media and politicians. We assume the worst of each other and demand that "the other" make concessions or conform to our perspective before being willing to engage in conversation. We want the oil to pretend to be water, and when it doesn't, we criticize it for being oil.

As Messianic Jews, we struggle not only with the Israeli-Palestinian conflict, but with all that it means to be an Israeli. Army service and the love we have for our country, as well as our precarious position in Israeli society, all come into play. It becomes more complicated when we think about the reality of our Palestinian brothers and sisters. If we were to adhere to the majority opinion in Israel, we wouldn't consider being in the same room with people who hold the politics and theology of Palestinians.

Being a country in crisis, Israel has tended toward the right in recent years. We swing right when we are afraid and left when we aren't. However, in our recent swing to the right, the left has become stigmatized. Terms such as "traitor" or even "anti-Semite" are attributed to those who self-identify as *smolanim* (Hebrew for "leftists"). Often, when Jewish people associate with Palestinians, especially to work toward unity or equality, they are labeled leftists. As Messianic Jews, trying to feel that we are a part of our country, it can be overwhelming when we are stigmatized for our political opinions ("leftist") and our spiritual opinions (followers of Jesus). Most Jewish believers in Jesus, therefore, avoid associating with Palestinians – Christian or otherwise.

The situation becomes even more uncomfortable when we reflect on our service in the Israel Defense Forces. The reality of the Middle East requires soldiers. As Messianic Jews, we are proud to do our part for the defense of Israel and to contribute to a country that provides the safety our grandparents did not enjoy in Europe. However, the Palestinians we meet have only encountered Israelis as soldiers at checkpoints, in patrols, and worse. There are inevitable reactions. Young Messianic Jews may feel guilty about crimes and actions they did not commit, leading to feelings of annoyance and pressure.

Many Jewish believers think, "If I don't want to be categorized as a *smolani*, and I don't see why I should feel guilty for serving my country, why would I dialogue with my Palestinian brothers and sisters at Musalaha?" In most cases, that is where it ends. But in some cases, something propels us forward – hope.

Those of us who engage in such relationships do so in hope. Despite all the guns, knives, hatred, and fear, we believe that there is hope for this land and its peoples that can change the hardest heart. That hope is the gospel of Jesus. His incarnation teaches us to look through the eyes of our enemy in the same way he wore the flesh of humanity. His death tells us to obediently hear the call to put ourselves aside and live for others first. His resurrection shows us that no matter what happens, God can redeem anything.

So how will this change our land? Well, Jesus changes relationships because he is a hydrophilic lipid, like soap, which allows oil and water to mix, as soap can attach itself to both fatty substances (lipids) and to water (hydrophilic). Yet when soap does this, it does not leave the two in the same form as it found them. Jesus can change our peoples when we are willing to meet him, have him change us through the process of reconciliation, and truly mix with the whole body of Christ.

Please pray for Musalaha and all those in this broken land who want to bring redemption and reconciliation through the powerful message of the gospel.

11

History and Narrative

From Musalaha's *A Curriculum of Reconciliation*

An analysis of the dynamics of conflict reveals important factors which may contribute to the continuation of conflict or to its resolution and reconciliation. Among these factors are history and narrative. This section attempts to define both, examining their similarities and differences, and especially how they relate to one another and the parts they play in conflict. We focus on practical examples of how Israelis and Palestinians express their respective narratives and consider the challenges posed and how they may be overcome.

What Is History? What Is Narrative?

Traditionally, history and narrative have been considered as two separate entities, although in many ways they cannot be separated. History is the study of the past, with special emphasis on written or recorded events (as opposed to the legends and myths of earlier, oral traditions), as it is generally believed that recorded events, or written "evidence," more accurately convey what actually occurred. History generally strives to be an objective, neutral, and scholarly account of the past in which evidence or historical facts must be provided to prove its validity, whereas in the oral tradition of storytelling, the *assumption* is that the story is true.

History differs from narrative in that, by definition, narrative is concerned with storytelling. The simplest definition of narrative might be: "Someone telling someone else that something happened."[1] While narrative tells, history

---

1. Smith, "Narrative Versions, Narrative Theories," 228.

has to prove. This is not to say that history does not tell, or that narrative does not prove, but generally speaking this distinction can be made.

Recently, however, the notion of history as a totally objective, unbiased account of events in the past that are unrelated to narrative has been challenged. Many historians, influenced by poststructuralist critique, have come to recognize the influence of narrative on history. For some, objectivity is deemed unattainable, and they contend that all we have are stories and myths. Others argue that even if absolute objectivity is impossible to achieve, it should be aspired to, asserting that there is still a difference between history and narrative, although the distinction is not clear-cut.

One of the most prominent historians to voice this critique of historical objectivity is Hayden White, who writes that historians "emplot" history, shaping it as a story when, in fact, it is not a story at all: "This is because stories are not lived; there is no such thing as a real story. Stories are told or written, not found."[2] The historical "fact," then, was not arrived at through historical research but was shaped and constructed. Thus, it is always possible for an alternative construct to exist. This is dangerous, for when there are competing versions, as there are in conflict, the outcome is usually decided by force. Whichever side is able to impose its own narrative or version will do so, while attempting to eliminate competing versions. Therefore, "power, rather than validity, is often seen as the factor informing choice among alternatives."[3]

As this debate rages among historians, most agree that balance is needed. Although history is influenced by narrative, and falls short of objectivity, there are differences between the two. Separate but intertwined, they are informed by each other, for one cannot exist without the other. History without narrative would be comprised of statistics and graphs, with no connecting story to contain them. Similarly, narrative without history would lack context, as it would be a story occurring within a vacuum.

While it may complicate our notion of history, narrative helps us understand the world around us, for "man is in his actions and practice, as well as in fictions, essentially a story-telling animal."[4] In fact, if we were to deprive children of narrative through stories, we would "leave them unscripted, anxious stutterers in their actions as in their words."[5]

The narratives we are told or that we adopt influence our identity on both the individual and group level: "[T]here has been a recognition that

---

2. White, *Figural Realism*, 9.
3. Rimmon-Kenan, "Concepts of Narrative," 15.
4. MacIntyre, *After Virtue*, 216.
5. MacIntyre, 216.

narrative is central to the representation of identity, in personal memory and self-representation or in collective identity of groups such as religions, nations, races, and genders."[6] This relates directly to conflict, for our identity is so inextricably linked to our narrative (and history) as a group that it is difficult to relate to the narrative, or truth, of the other side.

When it comes to conflict, one's subjective narrative almost always wins out over the less subjective history, since our narrative can be easily shaped in a way that paints us in a positive light. This is more challenging (though possible) with history. Also, narrative is directly connected to identity, and since identity is usually challenged in conflict, the unquestioning acceptance of our own group's narrative, in which we are the hero, often strengthens our identity. Political theorist Hannah Arendt said, "*Who* somebody is or was we can know only by knowing the story of which he is himself the hero."[7]

For now, we will focus on the narratives of Israelis and Palestinians. Obviously, each side is the hero of its own narrative. By examining the different narratives relating to the same historical events, we should achieve a better understanding of each side's identity and be better able to challenge both narratives at certain points. Furthermore, such scrutiny will furnish us with several principles about narrative in general.

Elements of Narrative

Both Israeli and Palestinian narratives are internally focused and contain historically accurate information, but the choice of emphasis is anything but objective. Both narratives "morally exclude each other and devalue and dehumanize their enemy's narrative. If the opponent's narrative is described at all, it is presented as morally inferior and irrational. The enemy is depicted as faceless, as well as immoral, espousing manipulative arguments."[8]

Narrative Provides Identity

Narrative can be a powerful tool to reinforce both personal and collective identity. Most national or cultural narratives focus exclusively on positive in-group images and place all blame for violence and conflict on the other. Both Israelis and Palestinians see themselves as the true victims of their conflict

---

6. Currie, *Postmodern Narrative Theory*, 2.
7. Arendt, *Human Condition*, 186.
8. Bar-On and Adwan, "Psychology of Better Dialogue," 206.

and view the other side as the aggressor, as each delegitimizes the other's perspective. This belief is maintained on both sides by the respective narratives of the historical past and is "proved" again each time the conflict escalates.[9]

Narrative Provides Legitimacy

Legitimacy is a crucial resource in conflict, with each side believing that losing its legitimacy would mean losing the conflict; and each side's "case" being built on its "legitimate" claims and grievances, which are grounded in its narrative.

> History is the reservoir of resentment, the fount of blame. History legitimizes; history thus sanctifies. . . . Without an acceptable recourse to the past, gaining legitimacy for rebellion and hostility, plus terror, is impossible. No contemporary cause, however implausible, achieves widespread following without such legitimation.[10]

For both Israelis and Palestinians, the proof of why they are right, and the other side is wrong, is found in the past to the same extent (if not more so) than it is found in the present.

Narrative Provides Functional Truth

Functional truth is partial truth that first and foremost serves a purpose (such as provision of legitimacy) and only serves the "truth" as a secondary condition. For example, the Israeli and Palestinian narratives both claim to be the definitive truth but are both one-sided, biased views. However, they do serve a purpose: each strengthens the claims and further entrenches the victimization of its particular side. A functional truth does not necessarily reflect a true history but rather describes a past that helps the group to function and even to exist. It is a biased, selective, and distorted story that omits certain facts, adds other "facts," and may change the sequence of events or deliberately reinterpret them. In short, it is a narrative constructed to suit the current needs of the group.[11]

---

9. This point on identity was adapted from Bar-Tal and Salomon, "Israeli-Jewish Narratives," 28–29.

10. Rotberg, "Building Legitimacy through Narrative," 1.

11. Bar-Tal and Salomon, "Israeli-Jewish Narratives," 23.

Narrative Leads to a Zero-Sum Mentality

Conflicting narratives may lead to a zero-sum mentality on both sides because the divergent narratives both deal with the same events and the same history, while drawing radically different conclusions. Any conclusion different from one's own is perceived as a threat or challenge, and since so much depends on the narrative (identity, legitimacy, etc.), if any part of it is challenged, one feels that the entire narrative is under attack.

> Palestinians and Jews each believed that acceptance of the other's identity would negate both their own case and their own identity. Each side believed that if it were to be considered a nation, the other could not be considered one. Acknowledging the other's nationhood was seen as accepting that group's right to establish a national state in the contested land, which in turn was believed to weaken one's own claim to the same land.[12]

Narrative Is a Collective Endeavor

A narrative account is not always literally collective, but when it concerns a people or group, it is by definition a collective endeavor, functioning like a personal narrative. In fact, the two often become one, as we connect historical events from the distant past to more recent events and to our own personal experiences. Therefore,

> the body of a collective historical narrative appears to entail both memories of past events as well as memories of more recent, conflict-related events. These more recent memories, some of them personal memories that intertwine with the collective memory pool, turn into historical memories the longer a conflict lasts. They exert a powerful force in shaping present-day attitudes, perceptions, and behaviors.[13]

As something collective, narrative is a unifying factor. This explains how Jewish people across the world, who have little in common, may all feel connected to the story of Masada. In the same way, Palestinians from South America to the West Bank are able to relate to the collective memory of the *Nakba*, whether they actually experienced it or not.

---

12. Bar-Tal and Salomon, 20–21.
13. Bar-Tal and Salomon, 23.

Narrative Is Selective

Both narrative and history contend with the challenge of selection. In both, selection is inevitable because an infinite number of things may be recorded. When recounting history this is typically seen as an obstacle to discovering the whole truth about the past, while in narrative, information is chosen to either glorify or vilify. While this process is deliberate, it is often unconscious. "The two narratives butt up against each other. They view similar events from different angles. They dispute the relative importance of the events themselves and the selection of the particularly chosen turning points."[14] No matter how objective we may think we are, our narrative is always colored by who we are. "Selection of details . . . and personas . . . , interpretations about motives, establishing the meaning of events within the general context, and even the tone of a narrative will always differ."[15] A key example is the difference between Israeli and Palestinian views of the 1948 war. While Israelis are quick to point out that Arab nations attacked Israel first, without mentioning the Israeli offensives, Palestinians usually emphasize the fact that Israel aggressively expelled many Palestinians from their homes and ignore the fact that Israel was in fact attacked by surrounding Arab nations.

Narrative Is Useful for Motivating and Recruiting

A collective narrative can be an effective means by which to motivate people and recruit them to your side in a conflict. This is similar to the functional truth aspect of narrative but more effective, for if a narrative can portray one side as the innocent victim, and the other as the aggressor, people will be more willing to support a more extreme leader and to commit acts of violence in the name of their people. They are also more likely to commit acts of injustice in the name of their people, which they might never commit in their own name, for "it is enough to say 'we' instead of 'I' – and we already have a ready-made easy conscience."[16] Narrative is a powerful tool for it "justifies the outbreak of the conflict and the course of its development. It outlines the reasons for the supreme and existential importance of the conflicting goals, stressing that failure to achieve them may threaten the very existence of the group. It

---

14. Rotberg, "Building Legitimacy through Narrative," 2.
15. Bar-On, "Conflicting Narratives," 144.
16. Buber, "*A Land of Two Peoples*," 170.

also disregards the goals of the other side, describing them as unjustified and unreasonable."[17]

Narrative Is Resistant to New Information

Whenever a narrative is created, repeated, and handed down over generations, it grows stronger and develops resistance to being challenged. The more often it is repeated (and, in conflict situations, it is frequently retold), the more it comes to be accepted as truth. Once a narrative is firmly entrenched, it is difficult to convince people who believe in it that they may not be seeing the whole truth. Any information that challenges the narrative is automatically rejected and labeled as lies and propaganda. "When members of a society strongly adhere to a narrative, which is typical in a time of intractable conflict, they tend to absorb what fits the content of the narrative and dismiss the information that opposes it."[18] In this way, narratives not only prevent people from seeing the situation from the perspective of the other, which is essential to reconciliation, but they also perpetuate the conflict. "Narratives evolve in times of conflict, and they also contribute to its continuation, which in turn reinforces their validity and prevents their change."[19] It is a vicious circle that can only be broken through awareness.

Bridging the Gap: Narrative and History in Conflict

It is evident that Israelis and Palestinians, like all participants in conflict, each have their own narrative about the history of the conflict and who is to blame. However, what is unclear is what should be done to achieve reconciliation. There has been considerable debate among academics as to whether it is best to bridge two opposing narratives by forming them into a third, joint, narrative to serve as the foundation for reconciliation or to accept that they will never be bridged and focus instead on pointing out the weaknesses in both narratives.

Some historians, like Ilan Pappe, believe that it is possible to bridge the gap between the Israeli and Palestinian narratives in several ways, such as by applying renewed emphasis on social and interdisciplinary history, rather than on political and military history. This would mean elevating firsthand, personal experience and witness accounts to a valued position. He also suggests

---

17. Bar-Tal and Salomon, "Israeli-Jewish Narratives," 24.
18. Bar-Tal and Salomon, 34.
19. Bar-Tal and Salomon, 40.

emphasizing the political and personal attempts that have been made by Israelis and Palestinians to work and live together in peace, with the goal being to "install in their pantheon of heroes and heroines, men and women of peace and reconciliation rather than generals and politicians of war and destruction."[20]

Other historians, specifically Mordechai Bar-On, have pointed out that bridging the narrative gap is impossible, if by bridging we mean reaching a point where both sides agree on what happened. He cites the example of the war in 1948 between the Zionists and the Palestinians as indicative of this futility, claiming that Israeli Jews will not be able to view it as anything other than the "War of Independence," which from their perspective, is "not only an accurate designation but also constitutive of the way that they perceive their entire collective existence."[21] On the other hand, Palestinians view the same events as a catastrophe, which is why they term it *Nakba* (literally "catastrophe" in Arabic), which is "an accurate designation of what actually happened to them, as individuals and as a collective."[22] Bar-On explains that not only is it unreasonable to expect this perception to change through bridging, but it is also undesirable to try to force the two narratives to blend into one. He objects to bridging efforts which, in his opinion, lead to "an attempt to reassert the 'truth' of one's own narrative against the 'falsehood' of the other."[23] This is not to say that historians have no role to play in the work of reconciliation. Indeed, they should seek to challenge the exclusivity of narratives in a conflict, while focusing on their own narratives, for "the demand that the opponent's narrative be revised adds to the strife, not to its resolution. Thus, scholarly confrontations between conflicting narratives can be fruitful only if each side concentrates on self-criticism, not on condemning the other."[24]

The following are several suggested points that Israelis and Palestinians might challenge in their own narratives.

The Israeli side can challenge:

1. The idea that Palestine was a land without a people.
2. The notion that there is no such thing as Palestinian identity.
3. The idea that during the 1948 war, Israel was surrounded, outnumbered, and outgunned; that it was "David versus Goliath."

---

20. Pappe, "Bridging Narrative Concept," 203.
21. Bar-On, "Conflicting Narratives," 143.
22. Bar-On, 143.
23. Bar-On, 152–153.
24. Bar-On, 153.

4. The idea that the Palestinian refugee problem was caused by Arab countries attacking Israel and is neither Israel's fault nor its responsibility.

The Palestinian side can challenge:

1. The idea that the Jewish people had no religious and historical attachment to the land.
2. The notion that Palestinians were totally innocent in 1948 and that only Israel and the other Arab countries are to blame.
3. The idea that the Zionists are to blame for everything that has happened in the conflict since 1948.
4. The lack of recognition of Jewish suffering as a result of the Holocaust.

Can the gap between the Israeli and Palestinian narratives be bridged? Should it be? And if so, how? Unfortunately, it is beyond the scope of this curriculum to arrive at a definitive answer to these questions. However, it is enough to ask them and to participate in the ensuing discussions. These questions will only be answered in the future, through the process of reconciliation.

And yet there are three steps that can be taken in the meantime, which will allow us to work toward reconciliation. The first step is "to know the narratives, the second to reconcile them to the extent that they can really be reconciled or bridged, and the third is to help each side to accept, and conceivably to respect, the validity of the competing narrative."[25]

Learn the Narratives

Since most people are already familiar with their own narrative, it is important to try to understand the opposing narrative. This is crucial because, until both narratives are known to both sides, there can be no relevant discussion. For many people on both sides of the conflict, just hearing the narrative of the other is a big step, for often they have never encountered it and are completely unaware of what it comprises. Once we are familiar with both narratives, we can listen to each other without being scandalized and attempt to analyze how the two perspectives differ.

---

25. Rotberg, Preface to *Israeli and Palestinian Narratives*, vii.

Bridge the Narratives as Much as Possible

As we have already seen, there are many obstacles to bridging between the two opposing narratives. However, this cannot and should not prevent us from trying. One approach is to focus on shared social and cultural history and to constantly challenge our respective narratives. It is important that we all work to challenge our own narrative, rather than tell the other side how its narrative should be challenged. This endeavor is supported whenever new evidence comes to light, such as the declassification of documents by the Israeli government, or the resurfacing of documents from the archives of Arab countries. While the process of bridging the narratives may never be completed, we can make considerable progress in narrowing the gaps between the two, which will help with the final step: learning to accept and respect.

Accept and Respect the Other's Narrative

Once we have learned each other's narrative and have attempted to bridge the gaps between the two, we can begin to try to understand. This is an essential step toward reconciliation, for while we may never totally agree on the past, if we understand each other's narratives, we will be able to better understand one another and develop empathy for each other. We may disagree, but if we know why the other side thinks the way it does – if it makes sense to us based on its narrative – it becomes much more difficult for hatred to develop. However, understanding is not enough. We must also accept the other narrative. This does not mean that we have to agree with it, but we must accept it as valid and respect the importance it has for the other side. As we accept and respect each other's narratives, we also feel acceptance and respect toward our own narrative, since this is a mutually beneficial process. In this sense, our identity is affirmed and a path toward reconciliation may be paved. This is essential, for, "in meeting the other, we do not deny our own reality, but seek to include the reality of the other . . . within our own reality, to integrate the other's story, point-of-view, fears, joys, and hopes within our own story. In confirming the other's 'presence' – or existential reality – we invite him or her to confirm our own."[26]

---

26. Paul Mendes-Flohr, preface to *Land of Two Peoples*, by Martin Buber, xvi. In his Preface, Mendes-Flohr is discussing the principle of inclusion in Buber's teaching on dialogue.

12

Fellowship: Breaking the Taboo

By Salim J. Munayer

Of the many aspects of reconciliation, fellowship with the other, with people we consider our enemy, is essential, for without it, there is nothing. Fellowship is the fruit of reconciliation and a symbol of its power and ability to affect lives.

For Israeli and Palestinian believers living in the conflict, the many challenges they face include differences in language, culture, and theology, and the physical segregation of their communities. Over the years, Musalaha has developed a forum where people from both sides can meet, establish relationships, and discuss their differences in the context of friendship. This forum has proven to be beneficial and fruitful, as many participants in Musalaha activities have remained committed to the process of reconciliation and to the friendships they have established. But, in spite of many successes, we are also aware of the external factors which complicate – and may even prevent – this process, such as the political situation, wars, and violence. As the conflict and discussions about the conflict intensify, dividing lines are entrenched and fellowship becomes taboo.

People on both sides bear the burden of proving their loyalty to their ethnic or national group. Recently, the theological and political debate has intensified, and a new dynamic has developed within the body of the Messiah: in-group pressure to avoid meeting with the other. Both Israeli and Palestinian believers have been told to avoid fellowship with each other, to refrain from the exchange of ideas, and to meet only with those who agree with their political or theological opinions. This pressure seems to be on the rise and can take the form of personal discussions, or emails and letters. The message is always the same: we are not to meet with the other but to stay within the bounds of our own group.

In this atmosphere of internal group pressure, two biblical examples come to mind. The first is found in the book of Acts, when Peter is in Jaffa and receives a vision from God. He sees a sheet filled with unclean animals descend from the sky and is told to kill and eat them. When Peter objects, claiming that he has never eaten anything unclean, the voice of God speaks clearly, telling him that what God has cleansed must not be called unclean. Then Peter is summoned by Cornelius, a Roman centurion in Caesarea. Peter tells Cornelius, "You are well aware that it is against our law for a Jew to associate with or visit a Gentile. But God has shown me that I should not call anyone impure or unclean" (Acts 10:28). When Peter returns to Jerusalem, the brethren have heard of his meeting with Cornelius, and his preaching to the non-Jews, and they challenge him, saying, "You went into the house of uncircumcised men and ate with them" (Acts 11:3). This was unheard of and was considered sinful. Forced to explain, Peter tells them of his divine vision.

This story has received much theological treatment, mostly focused on the issue of purity, and the dynamic of clean versus unclean. Commentators usually mention that Cornelius was uncircumcised and not Jewish to explain why the brethren in Jerusalem had such a strongly negative reaction to Peter's meeting with him. While this was certainly part of the reason for their reaction, it fails to recognize the fact that Cornelius was also the enemy. As a Roman centurion, he represented an oppressive military occupation that was resented and feared among Peter's people. Cornelius embodied the military might of Rome as much as its pagan gods. Therefore, Peter's meeting with him was not only a spiritual but a political betrayal of his people. Furthermore, to go to the house of Cornelius in Caesarea (named after Caesar, ruler of Rome), the seat of Roman military and political power, and share a meal with the enemy was, in the eyes of the brethren from Jerusalem, the height of treason.

The second story is found in Paul's epistle to the Galatians, when Peter and Paul come to Antioch. To understand this story, it is important to remember that the early followers of Jesus were deeply involved in debate over the controversial issue of how to relate to the new, non-Jewish believers in the Messiah. Paul's ideas were not accepted by everyone. Rifts were developing, and the situation was tense, not unlike today.

In this story, Paul explains how he had to rebuke Peter for hypocrisy. For while Peter had no problem sitting and eating with the non-Jews and having fellowship with his new brothers and sisters as long as the brethren from Jerusalem did not know about it, as soon as they arrived, he "began to draw back and separate himself from the Gentiles" (Gal 2:12). Why was Paul critical of Peter? Because he succumbed to the in-group pressure to exclude the other. As a leader, Peter's actions influenced others, since people were waiting to see which side he would take in the debate. As a result of Peter's weakness, "The other Jews joined him in his hypocrisy, so that by their hypocrisy even Barnabas was led astray" (Gal 2:13). The fact that Peter of all people should be guilty of this hypocrisy should tell us something about the difficulty of upholding one's convictions and about the power of in-group pressure.

The problem with the brethren from Jerusalem was not their zealous adherence to the arduous standards of the law, nor was it that they disagreed with Peter and Paul theologically. The problem was that they allowed their disagreement to interfere with their fellowship. It is no sin to disagree on theological or political grounds. Disagreements will occur no matter how hard we strive toward uniformity of belief. In fact, they represent the plurality of humankind's understanding of God's incomprehensible nature, each perspective adding richness and texture to the collective vision. However, as soon as we permit these differences and disagreements to obstruct fellowship, we are in opposition to God's will and his commandment to "love your neighbor as yourself."[1] If there was ever any ambiguity concerning the identity of our neighbors, Jesus made it clear in his parable of the Good Samaritan that our neighbors are the outsider, the other, the enemy.

It is no surprise that these stories from the lives of Peter and Paul revolve around the issue of eating with people considered outsiders. In the days of the apostles, fellowship was symbolized by the act of sharing a meal. This is why Jesus chose a meal to remind us of the sacrifice he made on the cross. He said, "This is my body, which is for you; do this in remembrance of me" (1 Cor 11:24). He chose a meal to unify us all as one body, saying, "This cup is the new covenant in my blood; do this, whenever you drink it, in remembrance of me" (v. 25). Fellowship is a sacred act, and if we neglect it there will be consequences: "For those who eat and drink without discerning the body of Christ eat and drink judgment on themselves. That is why many among you are weak and sick, and a number of you have fallen asleep" (1 Cor 11:29–30).

When we allow something to block our fellowship, we become susceptible to the sickness of hate and anger. To check the spread of this disease we must return to fellowship through God's love. Reconciliation is not an easy path to follow. It is far easier to surround ourselves with those who agree with us. But this is not what God has called us to, as we see when Peter slides back into his

---

1. Mark 12:31.

comfort zone so quickly and has to learn the same lesson a second time. This is because reconciliation, while a slow process, is our sacred duty as believers of the Messiah. We are commanded, through fellowship, to break the taboo of meeting with and loving the "other."

13

Obstacles to Reconciliation

From Musalaha's *A Curriculum of Reconciliation*

This section discusses physical, emotional, psychological, and ideological obstacles to reconciliation. The information provided is by no means comprehensive but focuses on the obstacles we commonly confront in our work.

Ideological Obstacles

Although ideological beliefs may also facilitate reconciliation, in this section we present those which obstruct the process. We have witnessed a number of different political ideologies that have influenced people to support racist and polarizing positions, like the one in apartheid South Africa. Political ideology often influences both emotional and psychological attitudes as well, which in turn become obstacles to reconciliation.

A group's *religious ideology* or theological understanding of certain biblical subjects can either encourage or discourage meeting the other. For example, believers may be encouraged to meet believers on the other side for the sake of fellowship and unity in the Messiah, while opposing theological understandings regarding ownership of the land or "chosen-ness" may separate people. While religious/theological or ideological differences between Israelis and Palestinians do not necessarily prevent them from meeting, it is often challenging when these issues arise.

The issue of *justice* can also be an ideological obstacle to reconciliation, with Palestinians who believe they suffer great injustice in the Israeli-Palestinian conflict perceiving this as an integral issue. Israelis tend to shy away from this issue, concerned about how it should be interpreted and its potential demands and implications. While our curriculum deals with the issue of justice, we have found that if raised too early, it may alienate one side or the other. Musalaha encourages discussion of this important issue within the context of relationships, after trust and rapport have been achieved.

Physical Obstacles

The most basic obstacle we face is the physical manifestation of the long-standing conflict or the *separation between Israelis and Palestinians*. Palestinians in the West Bank are separated from Israelis by a series of checkpoints and a wall (known as the separation or security barrier). There is less physical division between Jewish Israelis and Palestinian-Israelis (Palestinians with Israeli citizenship), although they tend to live in different cities or neighborhoods and have different opportunities. Musalaha contends with logistical issues, such as *finding a physical location for meetings*. When we hold encounters between Israelis and Palestinians from the Occupied Territories, the first question is *Where?* Israelis cannot go into the West Bank, and Palestinians over the age of sixteen cannot go into Israel unless they receive special permission. For our children's camps this is less of an issue since we are permitted to bring children from the West Bank into Israel for an event. However, this becomes more complicated when we work with women's groups, youth leaders, and young adults. Our goal is to find a neutral location where both sides feel equally comfortable or uncomfortable. Sometimes this is impossible. If we take a group to an Arabic-speaking country, the Palestinian participants are naturally more comfortable. If we take a group to a European country that is more Western, and more similar to Israeli society, Israeli participants often feel more in their element. So, while we strive for "neutral" ground, it is often difficult to locate. The most neutral ground we have discovered is the desert, and we generally hold our desert encounters in Jordan (or in the Israeli Negev for the under-sixteens). Far from civilization and physical reminders of our conflict – such as weapons, soldiers, and checkpoints – it is the best neutral location we have found for relationship building.

Misinformation, disinformation, and *lack of information* all constitute obstacles, while the third is largely the result of our separateness. When people have little opportunity to get to know one another, ignorance is unavoidable. In our one hundred-plus years of conflict, misinformation and disinformation abound. Sometimes the only reason for the incorrect information is that we have no way of knowing differently. Disinformation results when false information about the other is spread, whether deliberately or not. Sometimes people are unaware that the information they are passing on is false. Sometimes disinformation is willful fabrication stemming from the desire to demonize the other.

Physical *violence* is a huge obstacle to reconciliation. During violent periods (for example, *intifada* uprisings), dialogue, encounter, and reconciliation groups find it much more difficult to meet. This is related to the emotional and psychological obstacles of fear and demonization, which will be discussed later.

Emotional Obstacles

Some of the most difficult obstacles to contend with are the emotional obstacles within ourselves. Participants often become aware of these through their encounters with the other. Some newcomers to Musalaha are *suspicious* of the other side's intent or of Musalaha itself. At times, each side suspects Musalaha of secretly supporting the other side, so that dealing with this initial suspicion is often the first hurdle to overcome. Suspicions may persist, but usually, gradually, as participants get to know one another, they fade.

Suspicion is often related to *fear*. Lack of interaction with the other, or a previous negative interaction, may lead to fear of meeting the other due to fear of the unknown, of what one might be accused of, of antagonism, and of the reactions of people from one's own side – fear of being labelled a "collaborator." All of the above have led Musalaha participants to express initial fear or hesitation.

Another powerful emotional obstacle is *despair*. Some believe that the situation is hopeless, and it is futile to even attempt to address it. This is closely linked to *complacency* or *apathy*, as those who despair may choose not to do anything at all.

Hatred or *anger* toward the other may prevent a person from engaging in reconciliation efforts. Since tensions naturally occur along the reconciliation journey, even anger previously overcome tends to reappear. What is important is how the anger is dealt with.

The obstacle of *bitterness* is closely tied to those previously enumerated. Potential participants may feel bitterness toward the other due to things they have seen or heard and may thus refuse to meet. Often related to bitterness, feelings of *blame* about actions perpetrated against oneself or one's people may also stand in the way. Another deep emotional obstacle is *pain*, also a characteristic of intractable conflict. Both sides have suffered pain during the ongoing conflict and the pain itself, or the fear of exacerbating it, may lead some to refrain from taking part or to take a temporary or even a permanent break.

The two-pronged issue of *denial of responsibility/reality* may also prevent encounters. Some deny that their people have any responsibility for the current conflict and refuse to meet with anyone who thinks otherwise. Concern about "denying reality" may keep people away if they believe that engaging in dialogue or reconciliation is akin to ignoring reality and thus maintaining the status quo. This is a particularly important issue for many Palestinian participants who fear that reconciling with Israelis implies an acceptance of the Israeli occupation. Musalaha responds that it does not stand for the status quo but believes that the status quo can only change if the two sides work together.

Some refuse to recognize the divisive issues or label them inconsequential. While focusing on commonalities is important in relationship building, refusal to discuss what divides us prevents the honest, deep development of relationships which leads to reconciliation.

Another significant obstacle is the tendency to *deal with issues too quickly*. There are always participants who are eager to discuss the bigger and more sensitive issues at the outset. Since experience has taught us that dealing with these emotionally-charged issues at the wrong time may be too painful and lead to withdrawal before there is a chance to develop relationships, we facilitate such discussions throughout the stages of reconciliation, as trust slowly builds.

Psychological Obstacles

Psychological obstacles are prevalent, and often difficult to challenge, as people are often offended by the suggestion that they may have any. The psychological obstacles we generally encounter during recruitment or in the process of reconciliation can be summed up as *prejudice*. Before addressing common prejudices, we focus on some of the most common psychological barriers to reconciliation.

The first four are interconnected: *us vs. them ("othering")*, *moral superiority*, *ethnocentrism*, and *control*. Us vs. them, or "othering," occurs when we use social differences (racial, ethnic, ideological, etc.) to distinguish ourselves from others and view ourselves or our social group more positively than another social group. Moral superiority occurs when participants feel that they or their actions are the "right" ones because they have "better" moral values than the members of the opposing group. Ethnocentrism is tied to the previous two, as it is the belief that one's ethno-cultural group is more important than, and superior to, other ethno-cultural groups. Two sub-categories arise from ethnocentrism, namely *xenophobia* and *anti-Semitism*. Xenophobia is aversion toward, and fear of, those who are different, particularly foreigners, and can manifest as racism. Anti-Semitism is a specific form of ethnocentrism and xenophobia in which one feels prejudice or hatred toward Jews as an ethnicity, culture, or religion. As for control, some participants fear that engaging in dialogue with the other will cause them to lose control of the situation. Simply hearing different opinions, or having their ideology challenged, is threatening. Others worry that they may be portrayed unfairly or that the other side will gain the upper hand.

Dehumanization, which is related to moral superiority and racism, occurs when members of one group label another group inferior and express this through words or deeds. This may occur on an individual/group level or on a state level, if a minority group or another state is deemed inferior and discriminatory actions are taken against it. *Demonization* occurs when groups or individuals are characterized as evil. Both Israelis and Palestinians have been guilty of dehumanizing and demonizing the other. At Musalaha, we strive to counter the dehumanizing and demonizing attitudes prevalent within both societies.

Victimization occurs when someone is made a victim and punished unjustly or cheated. *Secondary victimization* occurs when, in addition to having been victimized, someone is also blamed for the situation. An example might be a rape victim who is then blamed for the rape and marginalized as a result. An example of victimization in the context of the Palestinian-Israeli conflict might be the situation of a Palestinian refugee who fled or was driven from his/her land during the battles in 1948, hoping to return. Unable to return, the Palestinian is victimized as a refugee, and experiences secondary victimization when he or she is blamed for leaving in the first place.

The *self-fulfilling prophecy* occurs when someone predicts a negative outcome and ultimately ensures (often unconsciously) that it comes about. For example, if an Israeli believes that all Palestinians hate all Israelis and therefore harsh measures should be taken to keep them at a distance, Palestinians who are affected by these measures are likely to come to hate Israelis, whether or not they originally disliked them. We often contend with skepticism and comments such as there is no point in dialogue, no point in meeting, we will never agree, and all efforts are destined to fail. Those in whom these attitudes are entrenched tend to abandon the process at the first sign of disagreement, believing their prophecy has come to pass. However, if participants are willing to listen to the differences, and begin the tough and painful process of working through them together, they will discover the points of agreement, learn to respectfully disagree, and realize the benefits of working for reconciliation.

Psychological *trauma* affects the psyche, and may lead to fear or anger, or a variety of emotions or prejudices which may become obstacles to reconciliation.

Prejudice

Prejudice is defined as an "aversive or hostile attitude toward a person who belongs to a group, simply because he belongs to that group, and is therefore presumed to have the objectionable qualities ascribed to that group."[1] Prejudices often develop due to a fear of being threatened in some way.

The extent of our prejudice toward others is affected by how strongly we identify with our in-group; the quantity and quality of our past contact with the individual/out-group; our knowledge of the individual/out-group; the presence of past intergroup conflict; and the difference in social status between ourselves and the individual/out-group.

The more one identifies with one's in-group, has limited contact with and knowledge of the out-group, and is separated from the out-group by a wide gap in social status, the more likely it is that one will feel threatened.[2] Awareness of these prejudices and willingness to face and work through them are part of the process of reconciliation.

The Contact Hypothesis

Contact Hypothesis maintains that the more we interact with the other, the less prejudice we will have toward it. Four conditions must be met for Contact Hypothesis to succeed: (1) The two groups must have equal status in the context of meeting each other; (2) they must have common goals; (3) they must have little to no competition between them; (4) and they must be supported by authority figures.[3]

In the context of Musalaha's reconciliation activities, we work to keep these four conditions in mind by trying to rectify imbalances of power between Israelis and Palestinians. For example, if one group is less informed about a subject pertinent to an upcoming discussion, we try to hold a separate session to remedy the imbalance of knowledge, so that both groups will come to the table on a more equal footing. As the majority of our activity is faith-based and revolves around working with two groups that share a common faith

---

1. Gordon Allport's definition quoted in Dugan, "Prejudice."
2. Dugan.
3. Gordon Allport, cited in Dugan.

identity, achieving equal footing is our common overarching goal. We focus at length on shared identity which enhances positive contact between the two groups. To meet the third condition, we hold mixed-team activities so that ethnic groups are not pitted against one another. While differences are discussed, competition is discouraged. Finally, we may ask each group's specific community (often a faith community) to support our reconciliation endeavors and to encourage their children, women, youth, and leaders to be involved. This positive reinforcement is necessary for sustained positive interaction.

Studies show that prejudice reduction is achieved through positive interaction with the other, personal relationships, the opportunity for open and honest dialogue, and a mutual commitment to reducing prejudice together.[4] We try to infuse all our encounters with these criteria, hoping that each one will be another stepping stone toward reconciliation.

Identifying and Dealing with Our Prejudices

The first step to moving beyond our prejudices is to admit that they exist. If we believe our prejudices to be justified, we will continue to treat others unfairly. We should consider those moral and religious values which warn against prejudice, even if moral and religious people within our in-group seem to be prejudiced.

The tests provided on Harvard University's Project Implicit website are a helpful resource for ascertaining whether you harbor prejudices. Prejudices are learned behaviors that have become habits and can be unlearned by developing new habits and/or expanding knowledge and contact with those we are prejudiced against, as explained in the preceding section.[5]

We can counter the perpetuation of prejudices by admitting that we have them. They may also be tackled through the commitment to try to counter them in ourselves and our children; to work with people who are different from us; to confront biases that we may not be aware that we have; and to change through a conscious effort to understand where our biases originate, why we have them, and then try to move beyond them.[6]

---

4. David W. Johnson and Roger T. Johnson, cited in Dugan, "Prejudice."
5. Dugan.
6. Teaching Tolerance, "Test Yourself."

Conclusion

As we encounter and learn to overcome obstacles to reconciliation, we hope for change. We hope that attitudes toward the out-group will change, which in our case means that Israelis and Palestinians will have greater appreciation and respect for each other; we hope for a perception of increased intergroup complexity – that as we come to know the out-group, we will realize that they have as many values, conflicts, and positive and negative traits as we do; and we hope that people will cease to view each other simply as products of their categories/groups. Finally, we hope that encountering and overcoming these obstacles will lead to an exploration and redefinition of our collective identities. While this does not necessarily mean that we will like the other group more as a result, at the very least we hope that it will encourage us (or our in-group) to be more self-aware and self-critical.[7]

It is important to remember that reconciliation is a long and challenging process. When one is frustrated, one should bear in mind that there are various stages to experience, all of which are part of the larger journey. Confronting obstacles and facing difficulties are a normal and necessary part of the process and not a reflection of success or failure. Further, in our experience most of the obstacles can be overcome.

---

7. Horenczyk, "Minorities and Intergroup Contact."

Stage Three

Withdrawal

14

Forgiveness

From Musalaha's *A Curriculum of Reconciliation*

Forgiveness means to release from liability to suffer punishment or penalty; to let go; release or remit; to cancel a debt in full. To cancel a debt means that you absorb the liability someone else deserves to pay (i.e. liability to punishment). Forgiveness also means to bestow favor freely or unconditionally that is undeserved and cannot be earned.[1]

Forgiveness, its significance and its implications, is a prominent topic of discussion in many religious traditions, as well as in the social sciences. Christianity, Judaism, and Islam have long discussed it, including how and why one should forgive. Motivations for forgiveness vary, and working toward forgiveness alone or engaging with others in an attempt to exchange forgiveness, "encourages people to . . . work toward authentic human encounters that hold the possibility of true healing."[2] Forgiveness may provide healing and may restore a relationship between two individuals or parties – or within oneself. English philosopher Joanna North writes, "We must overcome resentment, not by denying ourselves the right to feel resentment, but by forcing ourselves to see the culprit with compassion, benevolence and love, even while knowing that he has voluntarily relinquished his right to these."[3]

Forgiveness can be examined from a religious or non-religious perspective, and the general approaches are an intrapsychic/therapeutic approach, an

---

1. Cox, *Reconciliation Basic Seminar*, 89.
2. Clendenen and Martin, *Forgiveness*, 2.
3. Ceccarelli and Molinari, "Process of Forgiving," 239.

interpersonal approach, and an intergroup approach. The interpersonal approach naturally includes some of the methods of the intrapsychic approach, while the intergroup approach utilizes methods from both the intrapsychic and interpersonal approaches in its methodology. The intrapsychic approach will be explored here, and we touch on the methodology of the interpersonal approach within the intergroup approach.

Forgiveness is:

- A conscious and voluntary *unilateral decision* that "occurs with the victim's full recognition that he or she deserved better treatment," recognizing that the choice to forgive may not result in a response or repentance from the offender.[4]
- An intentional, active *process* which includes a change in one's emotions/attitude toward the offender, and a decrease in the desire to take revenge against an offender.[5]

Forgiveness is not:

- An emotion. Rarely do we *feel like* we want to forgive someone; rather, we make a choice to forgive and a change in emotions/attitude follows.
- Forgetting/avoiding the unjust act committed against the offended, as these are passive processes and forgiveness is an active process.
- Exoneration/excusing "that exempts the offender from the interpersonal and social consequences that his or her act deserves."[6] Even after being forgiven, the offender may still need to suffer

---

4. Philpot, "Forgiveness."

5. Philpot. Here are a few more definitions of forgiveness from various research journals: Forgiveness is "a willingness to abandon one's right to resentment, negative judgment, and indifferent behavior toward one who unjustly injured us, while fostering the undeserved qualities of compassion, generosity and even love toward him or her" (Hanke and Fischer, "Socioeconomical and Sociopolitical Correlates," 3); "In forgiving, a person overcomes resentment toward an offender, but does not deny him/herself the moral right to such resentment. The forgiver tries to have a new stance of benevolence, compassion, and even love toward the offender, even though the latter has no moral right to such a merciful response" (Subkoviak et al., "Measuring Interpersonal Forgiveness," 642); "Forgiveness will be conceptualized as a response toward an offender that involves letting go of negative affect (e.g., hostility), cognitions (e.g., thoughts of revenge), and behavior (e.g., verbal aggression), and may also involve positive responses toward the offender (e.g., compassion)" (Rye et al., "Evaluation," 261).

6. Clendenen and Martin, *Forgiveness*, 15.

the penalty for his or her actions, and/or make restitution to the offended.[7]
- Reconciliation, which is "the restoration of interpersonal trust in the mutual commitment to invest again in the relationship. The partners in a reconciled relationship do not fear the memory of the fracture, harbor no unattended resentments, are willing to be vulnerable with each other again, and permit the relationship to be different than it was before."[8] While forgiveness can occur without reconciliation, and the offended can forgive the offender without the restoration of the relationship, reconciliation cannot occur without forgiveness.

While some philosophical arguments oppose interpersonal forgiveness, most notably due to the claim that it can encourage further abuse, research indicates that contentions such as these misunderstand the proper definition of forgiveness,[9] and confuse reconciliation with forgiveness. On the contrary, forgiveness helps mitigate the effects of hatred and resentment that can lead to anxiety and depression,[10] and leads toward more internal peace and communal stability, as we will discuss in the section on intergroup forgiveness.

Understanding Our Complicity in Contributing to the Conflict

In previous sections we have considered how some things we cherish may be obstacles to reconciliation, may negatively affect the other, or may contribute to the conflict. Take a few moments and reflect on some specific beliefs, actions, or systems which you adhere to which cause or contribute to a conflict in which you are involved. This can be something seemingly minor, perhaps negative feelings or stereotypes within ourselves, or something that we have little control over, such as paying taxes to our governments, which (in addition to the good they do and services they provide) contribute to harming the relationship between our peoples.

While you or I may never have been complicit in a violent act against someone from the other side, as individuals and groups we have been party to offenses committed against the other. The American Christian theologian Gregory L. Jones elaborates:

---

7. Cox, *Reconciliation Basic Seminar*, 91.
8. Clendenen and Martin, *Forgiveness*, 15–16.
9. Subkoviak et al., "Measuring Interpersonal Forgiveness," 643.
10. Subkoviak et al., 642–643.

> People are not culpable for those histories in the abstract, as if – for example – I am somehow "guilty" for the enslavement of African Americans in the seventeenth to nineteenth centuries; but I am culpable for that history in the sense that the effects of slavery continue to mar my relations with others, making me complicit in the continuing racism of the culture into which I was born. I can either remain complicit in that racism, thereby perpetuating it in ways for which I am also culpable; or I can struggle against it, seeking to mitigate its effects. . . . But there is no one who can claim only to be a victim of others' histories; though levels of culpability certainly vary, sometimes immensely, we are all enmeshed in various histories and circumstances, and the result is that we cannot evade the truth that we all invariably diminish and destroy others in the ways in which we live.[11]

Theologians Clendenen and Martin comment:

> Reconciliation stresses that [we] consider the motives and patterns of behavior that result in the ruptures of trust and love in interpersonal relations. This . . . encourages people to deeply examine their ways of relating, their attitudes, and their actions, intended or unintended, whose consequences produce suffering. One's "unconsciousness" regarding free choices does not shelter one from responsibility or the consequences of the free choices. Critical examination also requires the individual to explore personal complicity in the larger structures and systems of society that demean or oppress or exploit either people or creation itself.[12]

Thus we see that while we may not be directly responsible, even as individuals we belong to groups or nations which are culpable to some degree for destructive actions against others. Being unaware of how we contribute to destructive actions does not excuse us from being part of oppressive, demeaning, or exploitive systems. In working toward reconciliation, we should be aware of our contribution to and perpetuation of the conflict.

---

11. Jones, *Embodying Forgiveness*, 62.
12. Clendenen and Martin, *Forgiveness*, 28.

Understanding the Function of Hurt and Anger

Sometimes our society and culture encourage us to suppress painful emotions of hurt, anger, and offense, relegating them to a position secondary to logic. However, feelings help us understand ourselves and create authentic relationships with others. Refusing to acknowledge anger or pain obstructs forgiveness, the deepening of relationships, and reconciliation.[13] Without articulating pain and hurt, we can never hope for its resolution. Protestant theologian Beverly Wildung Harrison writes:

> Anger is not the opposite of love. It is better understood as a feeling-signal that all is not well in our relation to other persons or groups or to the world around us. Anger is a mode of connectedness to others and always a vivid form of caring. . . . It is always a sign of some resistance in ourselves to the moral quality of the social relations in which we are immersed. To grasp . . . that anger signals something amiss in relationship – is a critical first step in understanding the power of anger in the work of love.[14]

She continues, "Anger expressed directly is a mode of taking the other seriously, of caring. . . . Where feeling is evaded, where anger is hidden or goes unattended . . . there the power of love . . . atrophies and dies."[15]

Intrapsychic/Therapeutic Forgiveness

The important *intrapsychic* (or *therapeutic*) phase of the forgiveness process occurs within oneself and describes the emotions we work through during the process. Some experts find this valuable and concentrate on it. Others, particularly those who work in reconciliation, argue that this inward-focused method does not have the potential to heal relationships or lead to reconciliation, given its essential non-relational nature.[16] While experiencing the forgiveness process alone is beneficial, it does not result in restored relationships or require that the offended engage with the offender, so it is not sufficient when the goal is reconciliation. The phases experienced in the intrapsychic phase, which are

---

13. Clendenen and Martin, 52.
14. Quoted in Clendenen and Martin, 57.
15. Quoted in Clendenen and Martin, 58.
16. Clendenen and Martin, 18–21, 44.

reflected in interpersonal and intergroup forgiveness exchanges, include the following:[17]

1. The Uncovering Phase – in which feelings of hurt and anger are allowed to surface, and the cause of the pain is identified, enabling the individual to move to the next phase.

2. The Decision Phase – in which, to mitigate suffering and a reliving of the offense, the individual considers forgiving the offender and taking steps to release negative thoughts and feelings.

3. The Work Phase – when the individual actively works to forgive the offender by trying to understand what might have led the offender to perpetrate the offense.

4. Outcome/Deepening Phase – now the individual realizes that they have gained emotional relief through the process of forgiveness and may even "find meaning in the suffering that [s/he] has faced."[18]

The first three exercises are not meant to excuse the offender, but to humanize them, to lead to the empathy and compassion necessary for forgiveness to occur. Additionally, the individual must accept the pain (not to be confused with thinking they deserved the pain), and realize that they bear an unjust pain, but will not allow it to continue to harm the self or others (including the offender). At this point the individual faces the challenge of offering goodwill toward the offender through "merciful restraint, generosity, and moral love."[19] This does not necessarily entail reconciliation, as the individual may not wish to meet with the offender due to trust/safety issues. Finally, experiencing the fourth phase may lead the individual to be more compassionate, and "the forgiver discovers the paradox of forgiveness: as we give to others the gifts of mercy, generosity, and moral love, we ourselves are healed."[20]

Intergroup Forgiveness

The intrapsychic and interpersonal principles of the forgiveness exchange are also relevant for groups. The following reviews a general approach to

---

17. The following four points are put together from Enright and Reed, "Process Model."
18. Enright and Reed.
19. Enright and Reed.
20. Enright and Reed.

forgiveness exchanges between groups, and briefly discusses academic studies from the social sciences documenting methods which aid or inhibit group forgiveness initiatives.

When dealing with forgiveness (and subsequently reconciliation) in groups or in a political context, it is helpful to remember that forgiveness is a collective act that joins moral truth, forbearance, empathy, and commitment to repair a broken relationship between communities or nations; that there is a fork in the road between justice and revenge; and that political forgiveness may prevent communities and nations from taking the path of hate.[21]

Keeping the earlier processes and steps involved in forgiveness in mind, we now consider several more aspects of forgiveness (some repeated, but from a different perspective) which are relevant in an intergroup context.[22]

Redeeming Violence and Suffering

> Redeeming violence is a spiritual, moral and emotional process that enables a victim to recover the basic elements of his/her humanity which has been stripped away through an act or acts of violence by individuals, militant groups, or the state. The basic elements of our humanity include our identity, sense of security and ability to trust.[23]

In a political or group context, often one or both sides have suffered violence and dehumanization as a result of the conflict. The experience of violence may entail physical, emotional, moral, or economic suffering perpetrated directly or indirectly by one party against another. This violence harms the way we perceive and interact with ourselves and others, making it difficult for us to trust (particularly authority figures), and often leading us to question our identities, our self-worth, and our way of life. The redeeming process takes place as we are allowed to express our grievances and pain, mete out justice for the victim and offender, uncover the truth of what happened, and reconstruct our memory by giving meaning to our suffering.

---

21. These three points are taken from Cox, *Reconciliation Basic Seminar*, 91, and his section "Forgiveness in a Political Context."
22. This point is adapted from Cox, *Reconciliation Basic Seminar*, 91–96.
23. Cox, 92.

Confrontation

> The path of confrontation includes empathic attention to one another, telling the truth of our experience without fear, and naming the wounding experience caused by another. A successful confrontation affirms that the other [side] does indeed care enough about the [relationship] that [it] will, in turn, risk listening and engaging in the pain and anger for the sake of the love. If the desire to set the relationship right is authentic, then the act of coming into the presence of the other, wounded as one may be, holds the power and the grace to effect the desired change. *Confrontation need not and is not intended to be abusively confrontational. Accurate empathic action is essentially a respectful conversation. It is overcoming fear or any form of retribution to speak the truth in love.* To lose the power of confrontation and to extinguish this capacity from the repertoire of human relations are to miss the chance at the best of authentic relational harmony.[24]

One of the first steps in an interpersonal, as well as an intergroup, forgiveness exchange is the confrontation between offended and offender. In a long-standing conflict, both sides have offended each other, and there is a need for mutual confrontation for wrongdoing. While often viewed negatively, confrontation is necessary for forgiveness to occur and the relationship to be restored. In the context of forgiveness, confrontation may be defined as "the direct bringing forward of painful subject matter."[25]

Repentance

> Repentance begins with a changed heart which results in changed thinking and ultimately, changed behavior. It means coming to our senses. True repentance requires a genuine sorrow. This means experiencing sadness because of the offense you have committed and the hurt caused to others.[26]

Often in conflicts between groups both parties must agree to change the behaviors and patterns that caused and contributed to the conflict. Repentance

---

24. Clendenen and Martin, *Forgiveness*, 60. Emphasis original.
25. Clendenen and Martin, 58.
26. Cox, *Reconciliation Basic Seminar*, 92.

is the appropriate response to confrontation. Repentance entails identifying and understanding your own actions and behaviors which have contributed to the conflict; feeling genuine sadness for how you have contributed to a breakdown in your relationship with the other party; making a choice to discontinue any harmful behaviors or actions; and adopting new behaviors or actions.

In many interpersonal forgiveness exchanges, repentance goes together with a confession or apology for wrongdoing, and once it occurs, it completes a forgiveness exchange.[27] In this intergroup forgiveness exchange, repentance is an internal process whereby the offender or offending group of people identify and begin to understand the effect of their offense on the offended party. It entails honestly looking at oneself and the wrongdoing and rejecting the feelings of remorse, regret, rationalization, and reversal of charge which corrupt a genuine process of repentance.[28]

Burden Bearing

> Burden bearing is the gracious and generous decision on the part of the victim to bear the scars of past actions by the offender which cannot be changed. It involves a choice to give up 'unforgiveness' and the desire for revenge.[29]

The next step in moving toward a forgiveness exchange in a group context is for both sides to consent to bear the burden for the things they cannot change. Burden bearing can occur when both sides tell the truth about what has occurred and subsequently identify the specific offense; and when both sides consider their own contributions to the offense, confirm the commitment to repentance, refuse to engage in negative attitudes and false expectations (such as withholding forgiveness until the other person earns it or withholding forgiveness without a guarantee that the offense will not be repeated), and finally, both parties redefine their relationship with one another.

---

27. See Clendenen and Martin's approach in their book *Forgiveness*.
28. Repentance is a part of Cox's methodology in *Reconciliation Basic Seminar*, and the approach to interpersonal forgiveness is inspired by Clendenen and Martin, *Forgiveness*, 68–76.
29. Cox, *Reconciliation Basic Seminar*, 93.

Confession and Apology

> A proper apology is one that acknowledges in a specific manner the hurt caused to another person, accepts moral responsibility and consequences, and offers a heartfelt plea for forgiveness.[30]

In this stage, the offender recognizes and admits the suffering and pain caused by the offense and is ready to apologize for it. An effective confession does not attempt to excuse oneself or shift blame.[31] Which confession you would rather receive?

1. I was wrong to have said what I did last night, but every time you bring up that subject it pushes my buttons.
2. I probably should have avoided what I said last night since you reacted so poorly.
3. I was wrong for what I said last night. I hurt your feelings and demonstrated insensitivity to you. There is no excuse for my actions that caused you pain.

Restitution

> [Restitution is] that which restores the injured party to his or her former position. It benefits society by making destructive behavior unprofitable. Restitution is appropriate both for personal injuries and for property damage.[32]

The basic principle behind this stage is the willingness to make restitution to the offended to demonstrate the offender's sincerity. Restitution should be made for physical damages. Pain, suffering and/or emotional distress are often too ambiguous to address concretely for the purpose of restitution. Damages can be divided into intentional and unintentional damages. Unintentional damage should involve repair or replacement of property, while intentional damage requires repentance, and restoration of property plus interest. Restitution shows the willingness of the offender to take responsibility for his/her actions and is beneficial to the offended as it restores what was lost. Additionally, it is

---

30. Cox, 94.
31. Cox, 95.
32. Cox, 95.

a physical display by the offender of the change in attitude and a commitment to the forgiveness exchange.

For Musalaha participants to complete the forgiveness exchange, it is important for both sides to realize the need for restitution but not to agree on what exactly restitution should entail. While negotiation is possible, exactly what the restitution will entail is not going to be influenced by the groups participating in the Musalaha encounters. Much will depend on the respective political leaders, and while we should contribute to the political process, there is no guarantee that our concept of restitution will be chosen by our leaders.

Closure

To complete the process, the offender and offended seek ways to restore their full dignity. Both remain committed to their agreement to change those behaviors that caused/contributed to the conflict, and the offended chooses to go forward, having accepted the offender's apology and agreed to bear the pain of what cannot be changed or made right by restitution.

When Forgiveness Is Not Offered or Accepted

When individuals or groups meet, and a forgiveness exchange is attempted, if one side refuses to offer or accept forgiveness, reconciliation is not possible. For reconciliation to occur, forgiveness is necessary. Our daily interactions with others, and what we see in the news, offer numerous examples of unforgiving individuals or groups.

In an interpersonal context, when an offender does not repent, it is necessary to draw a few other select people into the exchange and ask them to confront the offender alongside the offended. If the offender persists in his/her unrepentance, then, as a last resort, some Christian theologians advocate that the offended transfer the responsibility for completing the forgiveness exchange to God. Persisting in holding an offender responsible for an offense that he/she is unrepentant for will "only result in further victimization."[33] However, the offended person needs to be willing to complete the forgiveness exchange in the future if and when the offender is repentant. This process allows the offended to move forward "without condoning an unjust situation and enabling an unjust person to continue destructive behavior. . . . It changes our relationship with

---

33. Clendenen and Martin, *Forgiveness*, 113.

[the] offender and protects [the offended] from the negative and painful effects of continued engagement with an [unrepentant] offender."[34]

This principle is relevant to a group forgiveness exchange as well. One group of people will realize its need to forgive (and/or be forgiven) at a different pace from another group, and even individuals within groups will come to this realization at different times.

Research indicates that an atmosphere which encourages interpersonal forgiveness may lead to more internal stability within society. As forgiveness "improves wellbeing and decreases anxiety and depression at the individual level . . . we may conclude that similar benefits occur at the society level and manifest themselves in greater reported national-level wellbeing."[35] Consequently, encouraging forgiveness in communities will reap positive effects and "can be helpful for healing processes after conflicts."[36]

---

34. Clendenen and Martin, 95.
35. Hanke and Fischer, "Socioeconomical and Sociopolitical Correlates," 10.
36. Hanke and Fischer, 10.

15

Teaching Israelis and Palestinians Forgiveness

By Salim J. Munayer

Forgiveness is central to Christianity, and also to reconciliation. In the past, people from a non-Christian heritage have had strong negative reactions to teachings on forgiveness, as they felt others were imposing a Christian ideology. Many Christian and Jewish scholars have discussed forgiveness as it is related to the Holocaust, and in Israeli Jewish society, there emerged a saying, "Never forgive, never forget." While forgiveness was once a religious discussion outside academia, scholars now study how forgiveness relates to the wellbeing of humans individually and in society.

I recently delivered two lectures about forgiveness based on the research conducted for *Musalaha: A Curriculum of Reconciliation*. I talked to a group of Palestinian Christians and a group of mostly religious Israeli Jews from Bar Ilan University.

Addressing Judaism from a Christian versus a Jewish perspective is fascinating, and both the Christian and Jewish groups were challenged by our discussions. In Judaism, forgiveness is required conditionally in particular situations. In contrast, Christianity argues that forgiveness is unilateral and unconditional.

In Judaism, various schools of thought dictate whom to forgive, what it means to forgive, and when to forgive (Yom Kippur and several other times throughout the year). Rabbinical schools have various stipulations regarding the type of offense that requires forgiveness. Forgiveness and reconciliation overlap in Jewish teachings, as generally you forgive if the other person changes his/her ways; this approach does not assume that relationships are restored (as we do in reconciliation) but rather seeks to rectify the situation to maintain social order. In Jewish sources, forgiveness is considered important inter-communally, namely between one Jew and another Jew, but the same rules do not always apply between a Jew and a non-Jew. The universal obligation to forgive, a Jewish teaching of Jesus, is not embraced by much of the rabbinic literature.

In my lecture, I spoke with the Jewish group about Isaiah 53 and the centrality of atonement as it relates to forgiveness. Then we turned to Matthew 18 and examined how Jesus instructed his Jewish followers to forgive as they have been forgiven by God. The students had great questions, and we had a fruitful discussion on these subjects.

When I spoke with the Palestinian Christian group, I spoke about forgiveness in the context of the Sermon on the Mount, and we discussed how forgiveness is integrally related to the person of Jesus. Although many listeners are members of traditional churches and familiar with Jesus's teachings about forgiveness and loving our enemies, they repeatedly asked, "If I forgive, does that mean I let go of my rights and my desire for justice?" It is a good question and a common one for Palestinians.

This question reveals a common misunderstanding about the differences between forgiveness and reconciliation, so we deepened the discussion to define forgiveness.

We discussed how reconciliation is a mutual act in which both sides move toward each other – an act which includes forgiveness, but also accountability and restoration. Forgiveness alone may occur even if the other person is unrepentant. It does not mean that we necessarily feel happy as a result, that we forget the wrongdoing or excuse the sinner, but it does mean that we experience an intentional process to change our attitude toward the offender and release our desire for revenge.

These two lectures were very encouraging for me. At both, we examined studies about forgiveness between groups in conflict from Northern Ireland, Rwanda, and Bosnia and Herzegovina. Both groups found it enlightening to examine the importance of forgiveness in conflict resolution and reconciliation. It is an opportunity to move from a place of pain to a place where we take our hurts to God.

16

Fighting the Fear: What Are We So Afraid Of?

By Louise Thomsen

Every year we move our Palestinian summer camps to a new village or city to give more children the opportunity to enjoy a week of fun. This year, our eyes turned toward Hebron, the largest and most complex city in the West Bank (excepting East Jerusalem), with 160,000 Palestinians and 500 Israeli settlers, known for its violent clashes between the two. The Palestinian part of the city is exclusively Muslim and considered one of the most conservative communities in the West Bank.

Hebron was unknown territory for Musalaha and me. I had not been in Hebron since the outbreak of the First Intifada, and this camp would be Musalaha's first event in Hebron. I visited the campsite several times in preparation, but I must admit that I was fearful. I feared the unknown, feared being attacked physically or verbally for being a Christian, feared being met with hatred and bitterness. At the end of the day, it was a fear of Islam based on ignorance, prejudice, and stereotypes that I had built over the years, partially as a result of the growing Islamophobia in the West.

It seems that many countries in the West are encouraging its citizens to dread and hate Islam, resulting in the stereotyping, demonization, and dehumanization of all Muslims due to the actions of a few Muslims. The stereotypes have very little resemblance to reality. In my home country Denmark, the Muhammed drawings say it all. In this land, a lot of the blame for the Israeli-Palestinian conflict is placed on Islam.

This trend is also evident and increasing among believers. Often, we are told to distance ourselves from Muslims. We are encouraged to see Islam as a threat. I guess the road of battle seems shorter and easier than the road of reconciliation. The word hatred is not used but is there really any difference? There is also an element of arrogance, for we Christians tend to consider ourselves superior to Muslims who are often pictured as uneducated, primitive, fanatic, and violent. I think there is probably an equal amount of hatred between Christians and Muslims.

I also encounter this attitude at Musalaha events. Meeting with believers from the other side is one thing. Even meeting with non-believers is a possibility. But many are reluctant to meet and interact with Muslims. In recent years, Musalaha has initiated bridge-building activities with Muslims because we believe that we are called to do so, and many Muslims are eager to be involved.

I do not have deep theological knowledge, but I read in the Scriptures that we are to love everyone, pursue peace with all people, and be a witness to everyone. And we are told to do so not with words but with actions: "Dear children, let us not love with words or speech but with actions and in truth. This is how we know that we belong to the truth and how we set our hearts at rest in his presence: If our hearts condemn us, we know that God is greater than our hearts, and he knows everything" (1 John 3:18–20). Unless we make a conscious choice to educate ourselves differently, we inevitably grow up to fear Islam.

The camp for Muslim children aimed to love through deeds, and during that week my fears were put to shame. Through storytelling and song, we focused on five basic elements of friendship: loving, giving, trusting, being loyal, and accepting. We also painted some of the walls around the school, made turtles and other exciting things in crafts, built volcanoes and had coke squirt out of them, cracked open piñatas, and played teambuilding and water games. When Shakira's World Cup song blasted from the loudspeakers, everyone – children and leaders together – started to dance. We had eighty-two Muslim children, ages seven to eleven, join our team of fourteen local leaders and fourteen youth and youth leaders who came to help us from St. Peter's, Bolton (United Kingdom). It was the easiest camp yet because the children were so well-behaved and respectful – the best-behaved children at any Musalaha event. They were excited and grateful, and I did not hear any whining the whole week. Every morning when we arrived at 8:30, many children would be waiting for us at the school gate (some of them from 7:30, too excited to wait at home), with big smiles on their faces, greeting us: "Good morning, miss. How are you?"

On the last day, we invited the parents to join us for a farewell party and a viewing of the videos we filmed during the week. Many of the parents came, with a majority of the women wearing the burka and jilbab. They expressed gratitude for the camp, wishing it had been longer, and hoping we would return next year. These parents were not caught up in the Christian-Muslim conflict but just in the wellbeing of their children and their daily lives.

During the week, all my stereotypes flew out the window and were replaced with positive experiences and relationships which will encourage me to increase my interaction with Muslims and others different from me, just as God has commanded me to. I know that I am on controversial ground and some may say I am oversimplifying, but I believe we should share the experiences God gives us to help us shape our lives as meant by God.

17

Vengeance Is Mine? Breaking the Cycle of Violence

By Salim J. Munayer

I could identify the tragic evidence of the hundred-year Israeli-Palestinian conflict in his face. "All I hear about is saving my soul," said one of my students at Bethlehem Bible College. "What about the political situation in the West Bank? What does the Bible have to say about a situation like this?" He wanted to know whether the Bible had a practical answer to the daily violence in the West Bank. I had to do some study. It seems my vision, like many others', is colored by questions regarding prophecies about who has the right to the promised land. These debates have diverted us from God's commandments.

I had to teach my student three truths. First, God alone is the judge and the sovereign Lord. God said, "It is mine to avenge; I will repay. In due time their foot will slip; their day of disaster is near, and their doom rushes upon them" (Deut 32:35). He alone knows the hearts of people and how to deal with them. If we take vengeance into our own hands, we are assuming God's role. God will judge nations, as well as individuals. The prophet Amos declared punishment for nations which committed crimes against humanity in his first and second chapters. Second, God hears the prayer of the oppressed. Knowing this, David cried out, "Vindicate me, my God, and plead my cause against an unfaithful nation. Rescue me from those who are deceitful and wicked" (Ps 43:1). And third, since all vengeance belongs to the Lord, we must avoid retaliation. When we look at Proverbs 25:21–22, "If your enemy is hungry, give him food to eat; if he is thirsty, give him water to drink," we see that we are to return good for evil. In the second half of the verse, we read, "and the LORD will reward you." The word in Hebrew, *shilem*, means more than a reward. It also means completion. God completes the process initiated by the one who showed compassion to their enemy. This proverb invites the people of God to do good instead of evil and to wait for God to act. This does not mean the enemy will necessarily become our friend. Yet we must do what is right and leave the rest to God.

In 2 Kings 6:15–23, the prophet Elisha shows us how to deal with our enemy. The Syrian army surrounds the Hebrew city of Dothan. When the Syrians attack, God strikes them with blindness. Elisha tells them, "This is not the road, and this is not the city." He leads them to Samaria, and after they enter the city, Elisha asks the Lord to open their eyes. Looking around, they realize they are in Samaria. The king of Israel sees them and asks Elisha, "Shall I kill them, my father? Shall I kill them?" Elisha tells him not to kill them and asks, "Would you kill those you have captured with your own sword or bow?" He tells the Israelites to make a feast for them and to let them return to their master. They do as Elisha says. "So, the bands from Aram stopped raiding Israel's territory." We can break the cycle of violence by avoiding retaliation. But the conflict in the West Bank is more complex because we are dealing with a covenant of God. Both Jews and Arabs say that Abraham is their father and that God promised them the land. Isaac, Abraham's son, shows us a proper response to this conflict.

Genesis 26 tells the story of a famine. The Lord appears to Isaac and tells him not to go down to Egypt but to stay in the land that God promised Abraham. Isaac stays in the land, sowing his seed, and is greatly blessed by the harvest (v. 12). The Philistines become envious of his great prosperity. They stop up all of Isaac's wells and fill them with soil.

How does Isaac respond? In verse 16 Abimelech says to Isaac, "Move away from us; you have become too powerful for us." Isaac has the power to fight back, but he chooses to leave. He moves, and his servants dig a new well. There follows another dispute with the people of Gerar. Isaac leaves again. This happens three more times before Isaac is allowed to settle. Putting myself in Isaac's place, I would have had many thoughts: God promised this land to my father and me; he made a covenant with my father; I worked hard for this land; I dug a well, and without wells, I cannot live. Some might think Isaac was a weak person for giving in to the demands of his neighbors, but I do not think so. He learned something from his father – something Jews and Arabs need to learn today.

I may have a house, some land, and perhaps even a covenant. But if I am a child of God, will he not take care of me?

When we speak of land, we must remember that the whole earth belongs to God. If he wants to give me a certain piece of land, he will give it to me. More importantly, I have to be ready to die for him, not for the land. And if God made a covenant, will he not defend that covenant? That's what we see happening in Genesis 26:22. No one disputes with Isaac over his final well, so he declares, "Now the LORD has given us room and we will flourish in the Land." Then God appears to Isaac with these words, "I am the God of your father, Abraham. Do not be afraid, for I am with you; I will bless you and will increase the number of your descendants for the sake of my servant Abraham."

We read in verses 26–28 that Abimelech, king of the Philistines, comes up from Gerar with his advisor and his military commander. Isaac asks them why they came, especially since they had sent him away with so much hostility. They say, "We saw clearly that the LORD was with you." They now want to make a treaty with Isaac. They were afraid of what he could do to them.

By serving our enemy, we gain power – not power to destroy but to build, to overcome the hatred of our enemy, and most importantly, to overcome the will of our flesh. Jesus declared, "Blessed are the peacemakers, for they will be called children of God" (Matt 5:9). If you are a peacemaker, you will be rewarded with the status of being a child of God – the highest status a human being can achieve.

We must take seriously the command of Jesus to love our enemy and ask God to help us apply it to our everyday lives. Vengeance is not an easy desire to overcome. To love our enemy, we may need to pay the price of being outside the camp – the camp of our national identity, even our family. Only by the grace of God can we guard our hearts against hatred and begin to love our enemy.

18

Healing Brokenness

By Louise Thomsen

This year, our second national women's conference tackled the subject of brokenness resulting from experiences of the *Shoah* (Holocaust) and the *Nakba* (the catastrophe experienced by Palestinians dispossessed and displaced from their land in 1948). The purpose of the conference was not to compare but to understand the other side's pain. Though it exposed the pain of the participants, it was, by the grace of God, a success. The women had to achieve a level of trust that enabled them to listen to each other's stories of brokenness, moving them one step closer to reconciliation.

Each of us is broken. I am a broken person. You are a broken person. We can be broken physically or have a broken heart. An endless number of devastating and evil things can break us and fill us with bitterness, anger, despair, and hatred, which lead to self-destruction. You can be broken if your self-confidence is destroyed, by depression or loneliness eating you up, by a financial crisis, war, or conflict. Brokenness is a focal element in our everyday life.

We tend to compare our brokenness, seeking sympathy and compassion. Each person's pain and suffering are deeply unique and individual and seem enormous to that person. In Henri Nouwen's *Life of the Beloved*, he writes, "Each human being suffers in a way no other human being suffers."[1] Each person's particular brokenness tells us something unique about the person, so that sharing our brokenness with others deepens our relationship and brings us closer to healing.

---

1. Nouwen, *Life of the Beloved*, 87.

The Holocaust has broken the Jewish people. The *Nakba* has broken the Palestinian people. Horrible and unique events for both have caused some in both groups to grow angry and bitter, as hatred becomes the driving force of their behavior toward each other. As such, brokenness is a hindrance to reconciliation between Israelis and Palestinians, and one of the issues at the root of their conflict. We cannot reconcile with another person if we do not know his or her pain and suffering, and if we do not deal with our own brokenness.

At our conference, forty-five Israeli and Palestinian women studied the Holocaust and the *Nakba* to listen to and acknowledge each other's brokenness and to recognize and deal with their own, thus moving one more step forward towards reconciliation. It is not easy to face pain and suffering straight on, whether it is yours or someone else's, and many women felt anxious. It is also not easy to acknowledge the pain of others, particularly if your pain is closely intertwined with theirs, and you fear that acknowledging the other's pain will diminish your own. Nouwen writes, "The first step to healing pain is not a step away from the pain, but a step toward it."[2] We have to find the courage to embrace the pain, no matter how frightening.

Following lectures on the Holocaust and the *Nakba*, two guest speakers shared their testimonies. A Dutch Holocaust survivor recounted how she was forced to leave her home, parents, and brother at the age of six and flee from German soldiers together with her aunt and sister. A Christian family in Southern Holland hid them in their house until the end of the war. Her parents were not as fortunate. Her mother died of a simple illness after not receiving the necessary medical care. Her father and brother managed to jump off a train en route to a concentration camp, but German soldiers saw them and shot her father. Her brother managed to hide in a small doghouse until the soldiers were gone and reached a family that was willing to hide him. After the war, the three orphans were reunited.

A Palestinian woman shared the traumatic night in 1948 when her family, living in Beit Shean (Beisan), was ordered to leave its home within two hours or be shot by the Haganah (the Jewish paramilitary organization during the British Mandate period). With only a few belongings, they ran to the town hall where buses waited to take them and other Christians to Nazareth, while the remaining buses transported the Muslims to Jordan. On the way, they ate unleavened bread, and the whole situation reminded them of the Israelites fleeing Egypt. The girl thought she would return home in a few days and left her pocket money in a drawer. Sixty years later, she still has not returned home. An Israeli bank and playground have been erected where her house once stood.

---

2. Nouwen, 93.

The first night in Nazareth, they all slept on the floor in a big hall. After that, the Anglican Church took them in to live in their compound. They still live there today. She encouraged us, saying, "I cannot change the past, but I can change the future."

We were moved to tears as we sympathized with our sisters who had experienced such pain and suffering. I came to the conference with an idea of what our message would be – understanding each other's brokenness and pain. But God is great, and he had much greater things in store for us and a much more important message. The testimonies of the two women did not end here.

The Jewish survivor told us how she started reading the Bible, looking for answers. As she read, she realized the greatness of our God and came to faith. Shortly thereafter, she immigrated to Israel and married. Every year a German professor came to visit, and every year he encouraged her to visit Germany. Filled with enormous hatred toward the German people, she swore that she would never set foot in Germany. After refusing for ten years, she felt that God was calling her to Germany to deal with her brokenness, and today she is a free woman. No longer broken, no longer filled with the anger and hatred that she once felt were slowly eating her up and destroying her life.

The Palestinian woman did not deny that the episode remains in her mind and her heart and that it hurts to this day, but she has forgiven and does not hold grudges. Many still have hatred toward the enemy, but as believers, we do not have enemies. We were enemies of Jesus, who died for us and gave us life. This woman came from a family of strong believers and she firmly believes that the Lord had a plan for what happened. She met her husband in Nazareth, and for thirty-five years, they worked with Christians and Muslims. Today she is involved in reconciliation. She felt that the Lord was with her and the family through it all, and her message to us came from Romans 8:28, "And we know that in all things God works for the good of those who love him."

Instead of waiting for others to settle our hatred, we should deal with it ourselves by bringing it to God. Healing from brokenness comes from others, and also from God, and to seek healing we must seek him. While others must understand the pain, we do not need their apologies for our healing. These women did not wait for others to ask forgiveness, or for situations to change, but surrendered their hatred to God. They were set free, and today they shine as an amazing witness of the greatness of God. In *Mass* by Leonard Bernstein, it is written that a priest drops a glass chalice and says, "I never realized that broken glass could shine so brightly."[3]

---

3. Nouwen, 102.

We cannot allow the pain and suffering of the past to paralyze us but must try to change the present for the future. It is not an easy process. We saw how the lectures triggered strong, mixed emotions in the women and led to heated discussions and disagreements. We still have a very long way to go, and there is still much to learn about the Holocaust and the *Nakba*. It took those two women more than ten years to move forward, but they have shown us that it is possible to overcome hatred and anger. God never gives us more than we can handle. He wants to bring us near to him, but he sometimes needs to break us first. This way the suffering does not become an obstacle to peace but a means to it. It becomes a blessing. We are no longer victims. That, to me, is comforting.

Stage Four

Reclaiming Identity

19

Returning to Identity

From Musalaha's *A Curriculum of Reconciliation*

Identity is formed through a process of exclusion and inclusion, differentiation and identification. In conflicts, the differences tend to become sharp, demarcated lines that exclude others. In conflict situations, both sides often view themselves as "peace desiring" and the other side as "war mongering."

The polarizing differences separate us and may include elements of self-delusion and even infliction of harm. Failing to recognize our own shortcomings, we perceive ourselves as victims and tend to demonize and dehumanize the other. This section attempts to shed light on how these processes occur, and how we may overcome these challenges to our identities and embrace the other in our pursuit of reconciliation.

Identity in Conflict (or How Conflict Distorts our Identity)

A healthy identity allows space for the other; however, conflict often leads to distortion of our self-conception and perceptions of the other. Croatian Christian theologian Miroslav Volf writes:

> A tension between the self and the other is built into the very desire for identity: the other over against I must [sic] assert myself is the same other who must remain part of myself if I am to be myself. But the other is often not the way I want her to be (say, she is aggressive or simply more gifted) and is pushing me to become the self that I do not want to be (suffering her incursions or my

own inferiority). And yet I must integrate the other into my own will to be myself.[1]

He explains, "Instead of reconfiguring myself to make space for the other, I seek to reshape the other into who I want her to be in order that in relation to her I may be who I want to be."[2]

Exclusion means that one's own identity is affirmed at the expense of the other.[3] We make polarizing accusations, such as the peace loving vs. the war mongering, the good vs. the bad, the victims vs. the oppressors. This distortion is further accentuated when we focus on certain aspects of our identities in reaction to our situation. In conflict situations, we can place too much emphasis on our legitimacy and rightness versus that of the other side, and consequently we hear, "We are Jewish and have an ancient and ethnic right to the land; Palestinian identity is fictitious," or "We Palestinians have the right to the land because we have been here for hundreds and thousands of years; Israelis and so-called Jews have come here, converted to Judaism over the past several hundred years, and now make these claims on our homeland." Both reactionary statements are attempts to affirm one's identity at the expense of the other's.

How Conflict Leads to Victimhood

In the chapter titled "Obstacles to Reconciliation," victimization is mentioned as a psychological obstacle to reconciliation. This section deals with victimhood. While victimization occurs when someone is made a victim, punished unjustly or cheated, *victimhood* is specifically the perception that one is a victim, or the mentality that develops in which people see themselves as victims. Victimhood may entail the belief that one has little to no control over one's life, leading to apathy or stagnation. Generally, people who develop a victim mentality have suffered a wrong or aggression, but victimhood brings the victimization of the past into the present, and allows the person to be controlled or influenced by that victimization in the present. When discussing group victimhood, it is important to note that individuals in a particular in-group may embrace victimhood because they belong to a culture which embraces this mentality through its religion, education, and media.

---

1. Volf, *Exclusion and Embrace*, 91.
2. Volf, 91.
3. Volf, 92.

One striking similarity between Israelis and Palestinians is the mutual claim that they are victims of the other and the attempts of each side to prove it is the greater victim. This self-perception reveals the deeply ingrained victimhood of both societies.

In both Hebrew and Arabic there is no distinction between the words victim and sacrifice, *korban* (קורבן) and *dahiya* (ضحية), so that on both sides there is a close association between the ideas of being a victim and making a sacrifice.[4]

Israeli Perceptions: On the Israeli side, several victims/sacrifices are remembered in the Israeli historical narrative and collective memory. First, the state of Israel marks a yearly Holocaust Remembrance Day in which the Holocaust is discussed and its victims/sacrifices remembered. The educational system includes discussions of the Holocaust and anti-Semitism, and the Israeli media publishes regular items about the Holocaust and anti-Semitism. Further, those who have died heroically for the state of Israel are commemorated, most prominently in the context of the military, culminating in the national remembrance services held on Memorial Day. Civilian victims of Arab aggression from the early twentieth century to the present are also memorialized. The language and symbols used at these events exhibit characteristics of a society suffering from victimhood.

Palestinian Perceptions: The Palestinian historical narrative and collective memory perceives the Palestinian people to be victims/sacrifices from the end of the nineteenth century to the present, as foreign and imperial powers conspired to appropriate land for their own interests at the expense of the local Palestinian population. Israeli confiscation of Palestinian land is commemorated on Land Day, which specifically recalls the Israel government's plans to expropriate land from its Palestinian Israeli citizens but has come to symbolize the confiscation of Palestinian land in general. (It is commemorated by Palestinian Israeli citizens, Palestinians in the Occupied Territories, and Palestinians in the diaspora.) Additionally, Palestinian victimhood/sacrifice

---

4. Additionally, both these Hebrew and Arabic terms are associated with the common cultural terms for martyrs or those who have died for a cause, whether religious or national. In Arabic, the term martyr is *shahid* (شهيد) (a term both Christian and Muslim Arabs use), and like the Greek word "martyr," it means "witness," as a martyr or *shahid* testifies, through their death, to the truth of a certain religion or cause. While there is no single word in Hebrew for martyr, there is a distinction between the holy fallen who have died for the sake of God – *mavet 'al kiddush hashem* (מוות על קידוש השם) – and those who have died for a non-religious cause. For example, contemporary Israeli Jewish culture uses the term *halal* (חלל) for those who have died, usually heroically, during the conflict. The literal meaning of the word is "a void space," as if the dead are remembered for the empty spaces they leave behind.

can be seen in the marking of the *Nakba* of 1948 (and subsequently the *Naksa* of 1967[5]) in which Palestinians were driven from their homes and land, becoming refugees and suffering massacres at the hands of the Israelis.

The commemoration of these events focuses on the ongoing suffering and victimization of the Palestinian people, to the extent that it can rightly be called victimhood. Finally, just as the Israelis remember civilian victims/sacrifices of Arab aggression, so too, do Palestinians recall their *shuhada* or martyrs, both civilians and fighters, who have fallen in the face of Israeli aggression against the Palestinian people.

Social-Psychological Aspects of Victimhood

Social-psychological aspects of victimhood are reflected in a victim mentality in which an individual or group defines itself and is limited by negative circumstances suffered in the past or present.

Both sides are concerned with their "self-presentation as a victim, focusing on the unjust harm, evil deeds, and atrocities perpetrated by the adversary," and when "the victims retaliate and become perpetrators of physical violence against their adversary, a cycle of victimization and rationalization of that state begins to evolve."[6] The collective memory of wrongs suffered evolves over the course of an intractable conflict, and the commemoration of violence suffered and physical losses endured plays a role in furthering victimhood and perpetuating a violent conflict.[7] "As the number of human losses grows, societies develop beliefs about being victimized by the opponent. This self-perception focuses on the sad and wretched fate of the group, and frames its victims as martyrs. The dead and wounded become the salient, concrete evidence of the group's status as a victim."[8]

Victimhood breeds self-righteousness. Examples may be found in the media and historical narratives on both sides when allegations such as the following are made: "We never would have done _____ had you not done _____"; or "We had to do _____ to protect ourselves because you did _____." The cycle begins with each side asserting its community's innocence, or relative blamelessness, because the out-group's actions (in the eyes of the in-group) far outweigh the violence (or excuse the violence) the in-group perpetrates "in

---

5. Israel's 1967 war is referred to as the *Naksa* ("setback" in Arabic).
6. Bar-Tal, "From Intractable Conflict," 354. Also, Bar-Tal, "Collective Memory," 10.
7. Bar-Tal, "Collective Memory," 11.
8. Bar-Tal, 13–14.

response." Each side claims to be the true victim, and thus begins a competition to prove to the international community, as much as to one's own community, that one side is the "true victim." This necessarily delegitimizes the pain and suffering of the other. Further, the conflict-perpetuating victimhood becomes a form of power and influence that each side attempts to wield over the other.

Movement beyond the victimhood mentality is gradual, since this mentality allows us to feel that we have the moral high ground both individually and collectively and is extremely resistant to change. However, it is possible, over time, that we may begin to reflect on our own and our society's part in perpetuating this mentality; allow for self-criticism and seek to combat victimhood in ourselves; and challenge our community about victimhood's crippling and blinding effect and its role in perpetuating the conflict. We are hopefully able to identify with Reinhold Niebuhr's Serenity Prayer:

> God, grant me the serenity
> To accept the things I cannot change;
> Courage to change the things I can;
> And wisdom to know the difference.

To overcome an intractable conflict, a society must be able to change its beliefs. One element in the process is a reduction in "the monopolization of feelings of victimhood; that is, there should be a recognition that both groups were victims in the conflict and have endured suffering."[9] This is achieved by learning why the other side feels like a victim (learning its historical narrative), after which should come realization – recognition of the out-group's victimization and the in-group's aggression which has contributed to the conflict's creation and perpetuation. Recognition of the other's suffering and a willingness to move forward together allow the sides to slowly shed the mentality of victimhood. Finally, it is forgiveness and grace (seeing the other's shortcomings, choosing to relinquish animosity and bitterness, and allowing the other side to express its identity while accepting, respecting, and consequently legitimizing and allowing for differences) which lead to a reciprocal overcoming of victimhood.

How Identity Can Be Exclusive

Our identity is also formed by that which separates us from others. We often exclude because we want what others have and we want to be in control and

---

9. Bar-Tal, "From Intractable Conflict," 358.

have exclusive access to certain resources.[10] Exclusion quickly leads to violence, and conflict, and manifests itself in a false sense of purity in which the in-group views itself as good and pure in contrast to the evil and wrongdoing out-group. Exclusion can lead to elimination – whether through ethnic cleansing or encouraging the out-group to assimilate to the in-group's identity and values by surrendering its own. It may lead to domination and attempts to colonize, exploit, and subjugate the other for the in-group's gain. And it often leads to separation and abandonment when the out-group poses little threat to the in-group and the out-group has nothing the in-group wants or needs. Instead of helping to reduce the out-group's suffering, the in-group separates itself from the out-group so the out-group cannot ask for assistance.[11]

Exclusion is fueled by hatred and indifference toward the out-group and leads to a two-pronged distortion of identity (i.e. that of both groups). Furthermore, it dehumanizes the out-group while perpetuating the in-group's sense of goodness and innocence, resulting in what Miroslav Volf summarizes this way: "If we listen to what [the in-group] tell[s] us about its enemies, we are overwhelmed by the ugliness and magnitude of wickedness. If we let these same enemies talk about themselves, however, the ugliness mutates into beauty and the wickedness into innocence; the magnitude remains the same."[12]

This form of exclusion should not be confused with the necessary drawing of boundaries in identity formation.[13] However, these boundaries lead to exclusion when, in an environment of scarcity, inhabited by a plurality of actors with intertwined lives, the assertiveness of one confronts the assertiveness of the other, and the one becomes a perceived or real threat to the other. Mostly, the threat is not so much to the life of the other as to their boundaries and therefore also to their inner organization of self. This is the point at which the healthy assertiveness of the self often slides into violence toward the other.[14]

How Identity Is Challenged in Reconciliation

Meeting the other may be a challenge to identity in and of itself, perhaps because of what we know (or don't know) about the other. Encountering the other may cause fear and uncertainty if it challenges our negative stereotypes.

---

10. Volf, *Exclusion and Embrace*, 66–67, 78.
11. All examples taken from Volf, 74–75.
12. Volf, 79.
13. Volf, 63, 67.
14. Volf, 91.

As we learn about the lives of the other, and discuss history and narrative, we encounter new, unexpected information, which may undermine what we know (or think we know) about "how things happened" or "how things are."

Further, various elements of our self-esteem are adversely affected by reports in our media of what the other side thinks of us. Consequently, when we come face-to-face with the other, our hurt may rise to the surface and we may lash out in anger. When our identities have been wounded and we have been dismissed (or excluded) by the other side, our self-esteem is affected, and we naturally fear rejection. This rejection may be connected to a fear that the other wants to get rid of us, push us into the sea and kill us, or transfer us from our homes and livelihood. But more often than not, it is an emotional fear, which finds expression in our reconciliation encounters.

Learning to Embrace the Other

How should we deal with these challenges to our identity in conflict, and move from excluding toward including and embracing the other? How do we accept the other and adjust our conceptions about them in light of their otherness?

Righting Our Understanding through Repentance and Forgiveness

When discussing repentance, we briefly mentioned that both the offended and offender must recognize their complicity in the offense. While the grievances committed by both sides may not be equal, both sides must repent of their hatred toward the other and the offenses they have committed. Repentance of the victims, or oppressed, plays a huge (and often overlooked) role. Victims must repent of what the perpetrators do to them and of the fact that they often mimic the behavior of the oppressors.[15] Likewise, victims must "repent also of the desire to excuse their own behavior either by claiming that they are not responsible for it or that such reactions are a necessary condition of liberation."[16] For if they do not repent, victims cannot restore their dignity or bring any real change.[17]

They must repent the tendency to excuse their reactive behavior by claiming they are not responsible for it, or that such reactions are a necessary condition of liberation. Without repentance for these [failings], the full human

---

15. Volf, 117.
16. Volf, 117.
17. Volf, 117.

dignity of victims will not be restored and necessary social change will not take place.[18]

The offended parties can resist the hatred and harmful attitudes they harbor. "If victims do not repent today they will become perpetrators tomorrow who, in their self-deceit, will seek to exculpate their misdeeds on account of their own victimization."[19] Repentance will lead us toward forgiveness, which is "the boundary between exclusion and embrace."[20]

Coming to Embrace

Miroslav Volf describes embrace as "the will to give ourselves to others and 'welcome' them, to readjust our identities to make space for them, [and it occurs] prior to any judgment about others except that of identifying them in their humanity. The will to embrace precedes any 'truth' about others and any construction of their 'justice.'"[21] The will to embrace must originate in genuine sincerity, in the desire to move forward with the other, regardless of where they come from or any preconceived notions about them.

Volf outlines the four elements of embrace: opening the arms, waiting, closing the arms, and opening the arms again. To achieve a successful embrace, all four elements must be present. When we open our arms, we invite the other to be part of who we are and express our desire to be part of the other. We acknowledge that the other is not with us and there is expectation that the other will come and share our space. By opening our arms, we create space within our personal space for the other to join us, and indicate that our personal boundaries can be crossed as we open up so the other may enter our presence.[22] Finally, in opening our arms we extend an invitation to the other.

The second element is waiting. We must wait for the other, not pushing ourselves or imposing our will. We wait for the other to wish to reciprocate the action and open their own arms. This waiting indicates that while one side may have initiated the action, the goal of embrace cannot be achieved without reciprocal action.

If the other reciprocates, then we have reached the goal of embrace, the closing of our arms, in which we are both active and passive – we are holding

---

18. Volf, 117.
19. Volf, 117.
20. Volf, 125.
21. Volf, 29.
22. Volf, 141–142.

the other and being held. Here, we must be careful that we do not grasp too tightly and crush or assimilate the other into ourselves, as that would be an act of power and, ultimately, of exclusion. At the same time, we must not allow ourselves to retreat emotionally, and instead should give of ourselves in the embrace and allow ourselves to be changed by the presence of the other. In this act, we find affirmation and affirm the other.

Finally, for the embrace to be successful, we must open our arms again. We must not take the other into ourselves so that together the two of us comprise a "we," and our differences are ignored in favor of what we share. We must let each other go so that our otherness, difference, and uniqueness can remain.[23] We must step away and allow the other his or her differences, and allow ourselves to be "enriched by the traces that the presence of the other has left."[24]

For this embrace to be successful, we must first understand the fluidity of our identities and realize that who and what we are overlap with our individual and communal social settings. Second, when we embrace, we come together as equals who recognize each other; when we embrace, there should be no struggle in which the other is expected to earn our recognition. Third, the outcome is not predetermined: as we wait with open arms, there is no guarantee that the other will reciprocate and enter into our embrace. The other has the right to refuse our initiating gesture. Fourth, even after the embrace has taken place, no result is guaranteed. Any outcome is possible, but genuine embrace will not leave either side unchanged. This final feature builds on the previous two and is the risk of embrace.

There is always a risk when we open ourselves to an embrace as the outcome is unknown. That risk might involve misunderstanding, hostility, or violation and offense, and we may become either savior or victim. Opening ourselves to embrace is a gamble.[25]

Learning to Value our Common Identity

Another element of embrace is learning to see the other as different and distinct, but also as similar. This can be achieved by focusing on the common (or superordinate) identity we share, regardless of our multicultural, multiethnic societies. Psychological studies show that people gain self-worth from belonging to an in-group, and that learning to see oneself as part of a

---

23. Volf, 143–144.
24. Volf, 145.
25. Volf, 145–147.

superordinate group doesn't lessen one's identification with one's subgroup (whether cultural, ethnic, national, etc.).

There are a variety of superordinate identities that may be beneficial and conducive. For example, Israeli Messianic Jews and Palestinian Christians share a common superordinate faith identity. While culture, ethnicity, and even symbols and faith expression might be different, these two disparate groups share a common identity as believers in Jesus as the Messiah. Or, in Muslim-Christian-Jewish encounters, the focus can be on the shared identity as children of Abraham or heirs to the Abrahamic tradition. Research has shown that identification with a superordinate group aids in the maintenance of social cohesion and need not come at the expense of loyalty to subgroups (Palestinian, Israeli, Muslim, Christian, Jewish, etc.).[26]

These findings are valuable, for, in reconciliation encounters, participants often fear that focusing on a superordinate identity, or over-involvement in encounters which emphasize superordinate identity, will result in a weakening of subgroup identities. In fact, this dual focus on superordinate and subgroup identities, and discussion of subgroup differences, can strengthen relationships, allowing us to focus on unity within our diversity. Various aspects of our identity may be redemptive as we embrace each other in our uniqueness and differences.

In conflict, one may overemphasize the aspects of identity which appear to be threatened. This may be expressed in hyper-nationalist or hyper-religious sentiments where identity is reinforced at the expense of the other. Focusing on our common superordinate identity helps us see each other's similarities and consequently to appreciate our differences (rather than find them threatening), while encouraging an embrace of other aspects of our identity. For example, Palestinian Christians may feel that as a religious minority in Palestinian society, they must focus on their Palestinian identity to prove to their Palestinian Muslim neighbors that they are just as "Palestinian" as they are. Sometimes, Israeli Jewish immigrants may overemphasize their "Israeliness" at the expense of their former national identity. While the relative importance of various aspects of our identity is a personal choice, open to change, we should appreciate our multi-faceted identities.

Seeing ourselves as part of a superordinate identity grants us the respect necessary to hear and accept the way the other side defines itself. Just as we are complex individuals comprised of many identities – gender, religion, ethnicity, etc. – we can learn, through relationship, to recognize that the other is as varied

---

26. Huo et al., "Superordinate Identification," 40–45.

and complex as we are, which leads to healing and humanizing. Simultaneously, as our paradoxes, failures, and shortcomings come into focus, we gain the humility, self-criticism, and self-awareness necessary to continue our journey of reconciliation.

Conclusion

Reconciliation is not possible unless we are comfortable with who we are and can create space to include others in our identities. At Musalaha's encounters, participants learn about each other, focus on their common identities, and, in the context of relationship, focus on differences which enable them to be open to embrace. The challenge is to then confront the problematic and wounded aspects of identity. We strive to help participants learn about one another and the shortcomings of their own identities. Only through mutual respect, self-awareness, and humility can the reconciliation process progress so that we may reclaim, and stand mutually affirmed in, our identities in order to advance – stronger and more confident in who we are, both apart and together.

20

Imposing, Expressing, and Enlarging Identity

By Salim J. Munayer

Our identities are complex, and in many situations, we find that others want to impose an identity upon us. Yet it is more important to know and discuss how we see ourselves. In many cases, the way others refer to us is different from the way we refer to ourselves. In a conflict context, a discussion about identity can be combative, and we often find that people build their identities at the expense of others. As a result, identity tends to be the first casualty in conflict.

It can be overwhelming to see how many identities we have in our small countries. Our *Zayt* (Olive) group is mixed, comprised of Israeli Jews who are either secular or traditional, traditional and religious Palestinian Muslims, and Palestinian Christians. For a group activity we prepared a long list of identities: secular Jew, religious Jew, Orthodox Jew, Jewish Israeli, Jewish, Israeli, Israeli Arab, Israeli Palestinian, Palestinian, Palestinian Muslim, Muslim Arab, Muslim, Palestinian Christian, Christian, Christian Arab, Immigrant, Foreigner, Arab. One of the important points we emphasize during our meetings is that we should allow others to self-identify. This is an instructive activity because it allows participants to define themselves, and participants learn why each group member identifies as he/she does. It also reveals our diversity, for we are not just Muslims, Christians, and Jews, but many different types of Muslims, Christians, and Jews.

When dealing with different types of identities, external forces seek to simplify matters by imposing labels. In Noah Haiduc-Dale's *Arab Christians in British Mandate Palestine: Communalism and Nationalism, 1917–1948*, he discusses important issues faced by the Christian community as the British began to redefine religious identification; how the Muslim Arab leadership emphasized religious differences to increase power; and how religion became increasingly politicized and the conflict took on an increasingly national-religious character. The British tried to simplify the diversity and control the religious communities by dealing with them in three groups: Jews, Christians, and Muslims. The Christian community fluctuated between nationalism and communalism in its identity, always identifying with Palestinian nationalism, but at various points focusing more on communal religious identities as well.

In the *Zayt* group workshop, we divided the Israeli and Palestinian women into separate groups and asked each one to discuss its identity and set it down on paper. The Palestinian women drew a picture of an olive tree, Jerusalem, a *kufiyah* (traditional Arab male headcovering), and a number of religious sites. They wrote that their identity is comprised of religion, land, refugees, culture, existence, and historical/religious sites. The Israeli group, in contrast, wrote at length about what it means to be Israeli, emphasizing aspects they love about their culture, issues they struggle with, and more. One Israeli woman had a hard time expressing herself in words, and drew a beautiful sketch with many colors and interwoven parts. Afterward, I asked the women to think about what was missing in each of their identities. As is often the case in such interactions, when we discuss our identities we do not include the other. Commenting on the Palestinian sketch, an Israeli suggested that a Star of David might be added; the Palestinians were visibly upset by this. The Palestinians, likewise, challenged the Israelis about where they fit in the Israeli identity and noted how the Israeli version depicted its privilege. Whereas the Palestinian identity reflected basic human needs and desires, the Israeli identity comprised some basic needs, but also internal debate, self-reflection, and lighter conceptions of identity. The Palestinians were surprised at the prominent place that fear played in Israeli identity and asked the Israelis how they could be so fearful when they have the strongest army in the Middle East and all the power in Israel/Palestine. When the Palestinians emphasized that they could not give up any part of their identity, the Israelis were shocked, and one participant asked how, then, could there ever be peace? Later, I asked participants to choose the most important component of their identity. While the Israelis had different ideas, the Palestinians agreed that their existence and historical sites are the most important aspects of their identity.

21

Remembering Rightly

From Musalaha's *A Curriculum of Reconciliation*

Put starkly, the alternative is: either heaven or the memory of horror. Either heaven will have no monuments to keep the memory of the horror alive, or it will be closer to hell than we would like to think. For if heaven cannot rectify Auschwitz, then the memory of Auschwitz must undo the experience of heaven. Redemption will be complete only when the creation of "all things new" is coupled with the passage of "all things old" into the double nihil of nonexistence and non-remembrance. Such redemptive forgetting is implied in a passage in Revelation about the new heavens and the new earth.[1]

The Importance of Remembering

Intractable conflicts are marked by pain and loss, and when we meet for the purpose of reconciliation, we must examine how we remember the pain and loss we have suffered without allowing the anger, resentment, bitterness, and hurt which accompany them to divide us. Our reconciliation encounters rarely include participants who have directly inflicted pain. However, we are involved in a collective conflict, not individual conflicts, so our societies have grievances against each other which we carry with us, consciously or not. Memories of these grievances and how we have suffered at the hands of the other are part of our identity.[2]

---

1. Volf, *Exclusion and Embrace*, 135–136.
2. Volf, *End of Memory*, 24.

The question for us, then, is not *should* we remember the wrongs each side has committed against the other, but rather, *how* should we remember our suffering? And how do we remember the offending party or society rightly? How do we love the offending society – "love not in the sense of warm feeling but in the sense of benevolence, beneficence, and the search for communion," which is imperative for reconciliation?[3] When we remember the past, we allow it to come into the present along with the feelings associated with the memory (whether positive or negative). And, "since memories shape present identities, neither I nor the other can be redeemed without the redemption of our remembered past."[4]

The Shortcomings of Memory

Before discussing how to remember, we first need to understand *what* we remember. As finite beings, we cannot remember everything, and what we and our culture remember is selective and significant. Think, for example, of how victimhood was addressed in the context of reclaiming identity. Our memory is both passive and active. Sometimes we remember things that have no apparent importance, and other times, we *make an effort* to remember events or information. "We are not just shaped *by* memories; we ourselves *shape* the memories which shape us. And therefore, the consequences are significant; for because we shape our memories, our identities cannot consist simply of *what* we remember."[5] This is significant because what we (or our societies) choose to remember of traumatic events in our past influences how we think and what we do. *How* we remember the Holocaust, the *Nakba*, Israeli victims of Palestinian aggression, or Palestinian victims of Israeli aggression, shapes us and our societies. But since we remember selectively, and it is impossible to recall all the facts, we can be guilty of distorting memories, perhaps downplaying the part we play in offending someone or exaggerating the suffering someone else inflicts on us.[6] When ethnic and national groups' memories of suffering are memorialized, they are brought into the present and often projected onto current events.

---

3. Volf, 17.
4. Volf, *Exclusion and Embrace*, 133.
5. Volf, *End of Memory*, 25.
6. Volf, 68–70.

Redemption in Memory

To heal these memories and move forward, we should *name the past truthfully*, coming "to clarity about what happened, how we reacted to it, and how we are reacting to it now."[7] In situations of conflict, where both sides have suffered and perpetrated wrongs, we can only see a fuller picture when both sides are heard. For example, historical narrative is an integral part of this curriculum. We encourage participants to hear each other's narratives, and then we critique elements of these narratives. For example, we ask the Israeli side to challenge the prevalent perception that the 1948 Arab-Israeli War was an example of David versus Goliath – defenseless Israel against the might of the surrounding Arab nations – when an ill-prepared Israel faced the surrounding Arab nations and armies, outnumbered by the Arab forces dispatched to fight against it. And we challenge the Palestinian assumption that Jews have no religious and historical attachment to the land, asking them to recognize the connection between Jews and the Holy Land. While a painful process, when each side is able to question its own narrative and accept a new way of relating to it, it is on the path to healing.

Additionally, we have to *integrate the past meaningfully* into our own narratives. We often "integrate events into our life-story by giving them positive meaning within that story," and "we render the wrongdoings endured meaningful for us."[8] This proves to be therapeutic and provides an element of redemption to our memories. An example of integrating the past meaningfully can be seen in the early establishments of *kibbutzim* in Israel and the principle of Jewish labor. For years, Jews in Christian Europe were not allowed to own land, so with the onset of early Jewish immigration to Israel, there was a move to purchase land and develop communal settlements to work the land, reconnecting Jews to their biblical heritage. For Palestinians, it is common to meet individuals who are named for the villages their families were expelled from as a result of the 1948 Arab-Israeli War or the 1967 Six-Day War. This is a way some Palestinians look to the future and hope for the improvement of their people's situation.

Sometimes, when we have suffered terrible wrongs and can find no redemption in them, we must simply "*label* them as senseless segments of our life story. Once labeled, memories of horrendous wrongs are no longer loose beasts wreaking havoc in our inner being and external relationships; they are locked up in the basement of our mind. Though the imprisoned beasts

---

7. Volf, 75.
8. Volf, 76–77.

may stomp and shriek, we can live in the rest of the house unthreatened."[9] For Israelis and Palestinians, the Holocaust and *Nakba* (respectively) are often seen as terrible, unredeemable memories that can only be labeled as senseless.

While this helps us deal with the memory inside ourselves, to be completely healed and reconciled we must heal the broken relationship with the offender. And by doing so, we remember our wounding memories truthfully and therapeutically, motivating us to struggle justly on behalf of victims, and move toward reconciliation with offenders.[10] Coming to a place where we can, together, hear each other's suffering, name the past truthfully, integrate the past meaningfully, and label when necessary, can lead to healing and mutual affirmation.

Memory can be redemptive in a number of ways, when it is a means of healing, when a person interprets the memory in a new light, and when it is imbued with acknowledgement and the remembered offense is voiced and heard so the victim feels the injustice suffered is known and acknowledged. It may create solidarity, when society refuses to be indifferent and struggles with us against further similar offenses. And it may provide protection when society punishes the offenders for the wrongs committed.[11]

Yet the above is not sufficient in and of itself and can be potentially dangerous if isolated from the wider issues. For example, acknowledgment fails when the recalled offense is brought to light, and subsequently, the offended does not remember truthfully. This is not to say that the victim speaks about a wrong that never occurred; on the contrary, the event occurred, but perhaps the perpetrator's villainous role has become exaggerated in the mind of the victim, and thus the victim can do an injustice to the offender in his/her memory, and the public acknowledgement of the offense can be distorted.[12] Or, protection fails when

> The memory of [one's] own persecution leads to one imagining dangers lurking [which] may lead to the exaggeration of dangers that do exist, and overreacting with excessive violence or inappropriate preventive measures so as to ensure safety. Victims will often *become* perpetrators precisely *on account of*

---

9. Volf, 77.
10. Volf, 83, 131.
11. These are adapted from Volf, 28–32.
12. Volf, 30.

their memories. It is *because they remember* their victimization that they feel justified in committing present violence.[13]

Both Israelis and Palestinians have played the roles of victims and perpetrators and have often become perpetrators as a result of their memories of victimization and victimhood.

Truth in Memory

To come to a place of reconciliation and remember rightly, we must remember truthfully (as briefly mentioned in the previous section). But often in our telling of memories we change some things and summarize others as we remember only parts of what occurred. Although we are limited and subjective in our recalling and retelling, we can still "speak meaningfully of truthful memories. When we claim to remember, we are claiming that, to the best of our knowledge, our memory is true in the sense that it corresponds in some way to events as they occurred."[14]

As Volf comments, "Those who recognize the moral obligation to reconcile have, as a result, an additional reason for remembering truthfully. Above and beyond the fact that truthful remembering is a way to treat others justly, such remembering is an indispensable precondition of reconciliation between parties estranged by the transgression of one against the other."[15]

However, often in conflict the "truths" we are telling clash, for both sides claim to *possess* the truth and are more interested in this so-called "possession" of the truth than "the *moral obligation* of both parties to *seek* the truth."[16]

When we are so fixated on possessing the truth, it is impossible to even consider that there may be an element of truth in what the other side says, and we find it nearly impossible to be self-critical and doubt what we know. "Seekers of truth, as distinct from alleged possessors of truth, will employ 'double vision' – they will give others the benefit of the doubt, they will inhabit imaginatively the world of others, and they will endeavor to view events in question from the perspective of others, not just their own."[17] This is of essential importance when dealing with any difficult subject we encounter, whether it is historical narrative, conceptions of identity, theology, or memory.

---

13. Volf, 33.
14. Volf, 51.
15. Volf, 56.
16. Volf, 56.
17. Volf, 56.

Theologian Miroslav Volf, who has written extensively on conflict resolution, ethics, and peacemaking, further discusses this issue, stating:

> The purpose of truthful memory is not simply to name acts of injustice, and certainly not to hold an unalterable past forever fixed in the forefront of a person's mind. Instead, the highest aim of lovingly truthful memory seeks to bring about the repentance, forgiveness, and transformation of wrongdoers, and reconciliation between wrongdoers and their victims. When these goals are achieved, memory can let go of offenses without ceasing to be truthful.[18]

Remembrance and Non-Remembrance

The next logical question is what does it mean that memory lets go of offenses? What do we do with these memories? Do we remember grievances committed against us forever, and encourage others to remember our suffering forever as well? Or is the best option to set them aside, and forget them, lest they embitter us and our societies? And if we forget these wounds, putting aside these painful memories that have become part of our life stories, might that not sever a part of our identities, as part of our humanity is our ability to remember?[19]

Volf affirms the importance of memory, as "without memory, you could not be you and I could not be I, for we could not recognize ourselves or each other as temporally continuous beings moving along the axis of time."[20] However, he states that "under certain conditions the absence of the memory of wrongs suffered is desirable."[21] He describes his position not as forgetting and deleting memories but instead as "non-remembrance." It is impossible to demand that people forget their suffering; instead he offers a few principles of non-remembrance.

Volf suggests that wrongdoers do not deserve to have their deeds forgotten. If the wounded party chooses to forget, this is a gift of the offended to the offender. He writes that when we choose to give the gift of non-remembrance, we should do so not out of obligation but to imitate God "who loves wrongdoers

---

18. Volf, 64–65.
19. Volf, 24, 132–134, 147.
20. Volf, 147.
21. Volf, 148.

despite their wrongdoing."[22] He stresses that we can only give the gift of non-remembrance if we choose to forgive the offender, and the offender has repented and changed his or her behavior. While we can forgive someone who has not repented, we cannot give the gift of non-remembrance if they have not accepted our forgiveness directly from us. He also cautions that this gift of non-remembrance has limitations in our lifetime. We can only fully give this gift in the world to come, "where the wronged are secure, wrongdoers transformed, and both unalterably reconciled. Here and now, if we give the gift of non-remembrance at all, we give it only tentatively, haltingly, provisionally, and often with a great deal of pain."[23]

While memories of wrongs suffered play an important role in our lives, their main function is to act as "an instrument of justice and as a shield against injustice."[24] But when we wish to reconcile, we must be willing to give the gift of non-remembrance (as based on the aforementioned principles). At the end of the day, "only those willing to let the memory of wrongdoing slip ultimately out of their minds will be able to remember wrongdoing rightly now. For we remember wrongs rightly when memory serves reconciliation."[25]

Our sense of identity is not jeopardized by this because, while remembering is part of being human, we are who we are not simply because of what we remember but because of what we *do not* remember. Without an element of forgetting, we would find it difficult to understand anything. For example, to see a specific object, we need to focus on it, blocking out the surrounding objects. Or to listen to a certain instrument in an orchestra, we must block out other instruments in order to hear it.

Our perception and ability to remember are enhanced, in part, by forgetting that which surrounds what we are trying to remember, just as we often forget wrongs committed against us in our childhood by other children in our schools or neighborhoods.[26]

Do we remember so that we can forgive and reconcile, or do we forgive and reconcile so that we can let go of memories? We need both, in an unalterable sequence: in deliberate and often difficult steps we remember, we forgive and reconcile, we release memories. However, if reconciliation has not taken place,

---

22. Volf, 142.
23. Volf, 143. All content adapted from 142–143.
24. Volf, 149.
25. Volf, 150.
26. Paraphrased from Volf, 193–197.

the obligation to remember wrongs stands. For not only does memory serve justice; memory *and* justice serve reconciliation.[27]

Conclusion

In the course of our conflict, painful memories have shaped who we are and who we are becoming. But in reconciliation, non-remembrance and a certain type of forgetting play a constructive role in our perception of the world and our conflicts. To remember rightly, we must remember that memory is provisional, and we must be willing to remember in a redemptive manner and truthfully, embracing self-criticism and doubt when confronted with clashing "truths" and willing to see with "double vision" – from both our own perspective and the other's perspective. It is not an easy task, but it is a challenge we must undertake for the purpose of reconciliation.

> The proper goal of the memory of wrongs suffered – its appropriate end – is the formation of the communion of love between all people, including victims and perpetrators. Imagine this [chapter] as a suspension bridge in which the roadway hangs on a concrete arch anchored on both sides of the divide. The roadway is the reflection on memory. The arch that upholds the roadway is the process of reconciliation. The anchors that support the process of reconciliation are on one side the death of the One for the reconciliation of all, and on the other the hope for the world to come as a world of love. Perfect love is the goal of memory. And when that goal is reached, the memory of wrongs itself can end. Put simply, love is the "end" of memory in the twofold sense of that term.[28]

---

27. Volf, 204–205.
28. Volf, 232.

Stage Five

Committing and Returning

22

Dealing with Discouragement

From Musalaha's *A Curriculum of Reconciliation*

The Bible has many examples of discouraged people coming before God. Our spiritual mothers and fathers were no strangers to discouragement, and their stories, prayers, shortcomings, and victories are honest reminders of our human frailty before God and his faithfulness to us despite our frailty. The more you think about it, the more biblical characters who experienced moments of discouragement come to mind. Such a one, who encountered discouragement and still proved to be a leader until the end of his life, was Moses.

According to the story of Moses in the Hebrew Bible, he had a simple beginning, and after years of living in the courts of Pharaoh and then the desert wilderness, God appointed him to lead his people from exile into the promised land.

Moses had a daunting task and encountered challenge after challenge, contending with Pharaoh, Pharaoh's army, and the people of Israel themselves – with their complaints and their questioning of his leadership – not to mention the opposition he faced from his own family. He was doubted by those closest to him and had to deal with his own temper and frustrations along the way. His story is not an easy one.

Yet despite it all, Moses served as a model of leadership. He is known for his intercession on behalf of his people, even when they rebelled against him and failed to heed his words. He is remembered for receiving the Ten Commandments and for establishing the parameters of the relationship between God and the people of Israel. He is known for speaking to God face to face.

Yet Moses was human and responded to the hardships in his life with frustration and discouragement. In spite of all the great things he is remembered for, he is also remembered for his sudden outbursts of anger, for breaking the tablets, for failing to listen to God's words. As a result, at the end of his life, he and the entire generation he led out of Egypt failed to enter the promised land (with the exception of Caleb and Joshua).

The life of Moses shows us that a leader's life often includes pressure, frustration, discouragement, and loneliness. But as believers, we know history is not circular but is moving toward the purpose God intended.

Reconciliation participants encounter discouragement and challenges in the purposes God has set for them. As one seeking reconciliation you may be frustrated. You may fail God, yourself, and others. But as Moses shows us, we must press on and embrace God's command to be reconcilers (2 Cor 5:18–21). Each of us has a role, and God has a purpose for each of us.

The emotional toll of the journey of reconciliation is high, as opening up to express your opinion, hearing challenging teachings, and sometimes having your presuppositions challenged all require emotional commitment and engagement.

Yet it seems well worth the investment, as those who persevere beyond the pivotal point of "Who Remains?" often return with a renewed vulnerability and openness to positive change. The frustration and discouragement of those who bow out of the process can be disheartening, and we hope the examples in this section provide encouragement and reassurance.

Reconciliation calls for a change in the status quo, for truth to speak to power, and subsequently, spiritual and social change. It has an eschatological dimension as it calls for a hope for the future which it envisions in the present. The difficulty arises when people do not wish to relinquish their power or take the necessary steps for social change to occur.

Martin Luther King Jr, a leader who (like Moses) faced adversity, also stimulated great change and ultimately overcame immense challenges to inspire a better future. He played a political role, defying the power of his day, while pursuing love and reconciliation – seeking above all else to win over the hearts of his enemies. He faced many obstacles, was tempted by discouragement, but found the strength to persevere. Best remembered for his relentless commitment to nonviolence as he fought for the civil rights of African Americans, he was inspired by Jesus and Gandhi, and once said, "Christ gave us the goals, and Mahatma Gandhi provided the tactics."[1] He was moved by Jesus's teachings in his Sermon on the Mount and Gandhi's implementation of these very teachings in India, saying, "Gandhi was probably

---

1. Corretta Scott King, "Introduction," *Strength to Love*, 7. Corretta Scott King was the wife of Martin Luther King Jr.

the first person in history to lift the love ethic of Jesus above mere interaction between individuals to a powerful and effective social force on a large scale."[2]

Practical Steps for Dealing with Discouragement

One should anticipate discouragement and opposition to reconciliation, and if you are prepared for it, it will be easier to face. It is vital to remember that your vision and goal is reconciliation. Focus as much as you can on the "big picture." Through reflection, contemplation, and prayer, take time to remember why you are involved. It is helpful to think about inspirational figures like Martin Luther King Jr. Remembering how others dealt with trying situations, suffered setbacks, and persevered to eventually overcome obstacles is encouraging and often renews motivation. It is important to stay connected with other people involved in reconciliation and make time for the relationships you have established. Having an outlet to express successes, challenges, and frustrations throughout the reconciliation journey is a vital part of staying involved in the process. Follow-ups provide this to an extent, but participating in a more frequent forum is also necessary. This may be found in relationships with others involved in the reconciliation process and meeting or talking on a regular basis.

A further tip is to reflect upon what you have accomplished throughout your personal reconciliation journey – how you have changed; perhaps how you have influenced others to change; relationships you have established; and the positive effects these have had on you and others. Finally, take time to do things you enjoy. Reconciliation is one goal we are striving toward, but we all have other goals and efforts we are involved in, personally, in our families, and in our faith communities. No one goal should become the sole focus of our energy and life, or we will neglect other emotional, spiritual, and social needs.

Conclusion

Reconciliation participants and leaders will deal with feelings, and periods, of discouragement, as all people do at times in most aspects of their lives. Reconciliation urges a change in our hearts and in our societies. When there is no immediate change in society, we may feel that we are failing. As mentioned above, a balanced attitude toward discouragement, and the tools to deal with it, will enable you to continue your journey of reconciliation and help others in the process as well.

---

2. Martin Luther King Jr, "Martin Luther King."

23

Patient Hope for Reconciliation

By Hadassa, Musalaha Participant

When visiting Canterbury Cathedral during a school trip in sixth grade, I could never have imagined that one day I'd find myself in the West Bank, in a room full of local women discussing reconciliation with the archbishop's wife.

Life throws funny surprises at you sometimes, especially in this part of the world, and that is exactly what happened when I was asked to join a diverse group of Musalaha women from Israel and Palestine. For security reasons, the identity of the guest of honor was not revealed in advance. We were only told that she was from England, and we should be absolutely punctual and dress the part.

Shortly before the meeting we learned that we were about to meet Mrs Caroline Welby, wife of the Most Reverend and Right Honorable Justin Welby, the Lord Archbishop of Canterbury and head of the Anglican Church. The couple was traveling the Holy Land on a ten-day trip to meet with spiritual and political leaders, visit churches, local communities and NGOs, and hold interfaith meetings.

A quick Internet search revealed that the archbishop is a very special man. For starters, even before his visit, he clarified that he wasn't visiting Israel to push a political agenda, telling the BBC that he was coming, "To pray, to share, to encourage," as, "You cannot, in a place as complicated as this, go and lecture people."[1]

No stranger to reconciliation, he made a historic move by inviting his personal friend, UK Chief Rabbi Ephraim Mirvis, to join him on the trip.

---

1. Yolande Knell, 8 May 2017. BBC, "Archbishop of Canterbury to Meet Palestinian and Israeli Leaders," https://www.bbc.com/news/uk-39843985.

The two prayed side by side for peace at the Western Wall, visited the Yad Vashem Holocaust Museum together, and paid tribute to the British student Hannah Bladon who had been murdered in a terror attack the month before. The Archbishop and his wife continued to a kibbutz, listened to the life story of a Holocaust survivor, and met with Palestinian farmers affected by the Israeli separation wall. He even visited the Gaza Strip. It was a rare opportunity for Musalaha to be included in this busy schedule for a "Celebration of Reconciliation" in Beit Jala!

Accompanied by her local host, Mrs Shafeeqa Dawani, Mrs Welby, the Archbishop's wife, met our group in Jerusalem with her team, which included Canon Sarah Snyder, the Archbishop's Advisor for Reconciliation, and Kat Brealey, Presence and Engagement National Program Coordinator.

Anticipating that the meeting would be more formal than spiritual, I was positively surprised when we were each asked to prepare a Bible verse that connects us to the work of Musalaha. Reflecting on the Scriptures was very enriching, as we all shared different insights about well-known verses like Ephesians 2:14, Matthew 5:9, and 2 Corinthians 5:18–19.

Our time of fellowship included a worship session with songs in Hebrew, Arabic, and English, and a time of sharing about our role as women in areas of conflict. Mrs Welby provided heartfelt words of encouragement, and Canon Snyder shared a message about the cross and how it reconciles us not only with Jesus but also with others through him and his sacrifice.

The atmosphere throughout the meeting was one of shared spirituality and sisterhood which also enabled discussion about the daily challenges in the region. A conversation with Mrs Dawani was especially significant. As wife of the Archbishop in Jerusalem, she is a person of influence in the Palestinian church, but other than by name she didn't know about Musalaha. She spoke honestly, raising important questions about the challenging nature of the call to reconciliation, particularly for those in her own community who risk harsh criticism for engaging with Israelis. She listened intently as Musalaha staff Hedva Haymov, Shireen Awwad Hillal, and others responded to her questions from their own experience of these trials.

After concluding the meeting with a recitation of the Coventry Litany of Reconciliation, as our guests enjoyed refreshments, Kat Brealey provided words of encouragement, saying that although we aren't always aware that we're making progress, we are doing important groundwork. When the time for a peace agreement comes, people like us, whose hearts are already open, will be needed no less than today to reach out to our fellow sisters and brothers.

24

Justice from a Biblical Perspective

From Musalaha's *A Curriculum of Reconciliation*

Forgiveness and power have already been discussed, and they should also be understood in the context of justice. To speak of justice implies that injustice exists, and injustice hints at conflict. Justice is crucial to conflict, conflict resolution, and reconciliation. We begin by exploring justice from a biblical perspective and progress to an analysis of justice and reconciliation and the interplay between the two. We examine biblical justice and its relation to conflict, and how modern interpretations of justice have been influenced by the biblical concept, noting which aspects of biblical justice have been preserved and which ignored.

In one of the most well-known passages from the Bible concerning justice, the prophet Amos writes, "Let justice roll on like a river, righteousness like a never-failing stream!" (Amos 5:24). This image of justice differs from the modern, Western conception, usually represented by a scale weighing two sides objectively, in a detached manner. In the Bible, justice is not a static or universally applicable ethical theory but a dynamic and powerful force, complex and multi-faceted, surging ahead and adapting to new situations. While there is no single, conclusive definition of biblical justice, we can glean understanding about what it seeks to accomplish and learn about its life-changing power.

Biblical Justice: Some Terms

Two Hebrew words used to describe justice in the Old Testament are *tsedeq* and *mishpat*, each of which reveals a different nuance to deepen our understanding.

Tsedeq is understood as acquittal, deliverance, judgment, justice, salvation, help, vindication, order (in creation), and community loyalty. *Mishpat* is understood as vindication of the oppressed, requital, vengeance, or the retributive justice of God.[1] *Tsedeq* and *mishpat* are also related to *shalom*, or peace, and relate to each other in terms of covenant. The covenant is between God and humankind, with *shalom* representing the correct structure of the human community that allows us to benefit from God's commitment to support and protect it. In the same way, *tsedeq* represents the covenant in that it provides the guidelines for living according to *shalom*. Also connected to this concept of covenant is *hesed*, or mercy. With these three ideas in mind, *tsedeq*, *shalom*, and *hesed*, we understand the covenant that God had with the children of Israel in the Old Testament: "Generally, the righteous person in Israel is the one who preserves the peace and wholeness of the community by fulfilling the demands of communal living."[2]

This covenant is not limited to the Old Testament, for the life and teaching of Jesus constantly illustrated and expanded this covenant beyond the borders of the children of Israel. For example, the parable of the Good Samaritan

> would have been shocking to its hearers because those characters in the parable who would have been expected to be *tsaddiq* [righteous] were not, and the Samaritan, one clearly outside the covenant for the hearers, is the one person who is *tsaddiq*. The parable thus opens the way to reflection on who is *tsaddiq* and who is part of the covenant.[3]

This is a theme taken up by Paul; God's mercy (and through it, his peace, justice, and righteousness) is extended to everyone who is a child of God, even those outside his covenant.[4]

The Attributes of Justice
Justice as Restitution/Repayment

In Exodus 22, there are a number of statements detailing how an offender should "make restitution" for an injustice he or she has caused, whether it is theft of or damage to another's property. Isaiah 59:17–18 portrays a righteous

---

1. Definitions of *tsedeq* and *mishpat* come from Regehr, "Justice and Forgiveness."
2. Toews, *Romans*, 401.
3. Regehr, "Justice and Forgiveness," 48.
4. Ephesians 2:1–4.

God who repays evil doers with his wrath. The word used here is *shalem* (repay). It is used differently in Joel 2:23–25, where God repays his people with his mercy after the damage caused by his punishment. "In an act of mercy for the offender, peace (*shalom*) is the repayment (*shillum*) that God offers."[5] In Psalm 62:12, the word *shalem* suggests repayment for behavior, whether good or evil. This repayment is an expression of God's mercy and faithfulness to the covenant. This is quite different from Jesus's parable of the laborers in the vineyard in Matthew 20:14–15. In this story, the laborers are paid the same amount although they did not work for the same length of time. This is repayment based on God's mercy and generosity, not on the behavior of the laborers.

Justice as Vindication/Vengeance

Justice is also related to *naqam* (revenge), which can be seen as God wreaking vengeance on the oppressors on behalf of the oppressed. The numerous examples in the Bible include vindication. As oppression was often perceived as punishment for sinful behavior, the acts of liberation and vengeance are also a testament to the innocence of the oppressed. An example is the slavery suffered by the children of Israel in Egypt. It is important to distinguish between vindication/vengeance and vindictiveness. Vindication is an act of judgment which demonstrates that the oppressor is in the wrong. Vengeance is a form of justice-inspired harm caused to the offender, with the intention of bringing about a change and bringing about justice. Vindictiveness, on the other hand, is the desire to cause harm for the sake of harm. In the New Testament these concepts change. In Romans 12:17–19, Paul warns us to avoid vengeance and leave it to God. We are urged to forgive and told that our vindication will arrive with God's final judgment.

Justice as Retribution/Punishment

When justice is related to retribution and punishment, it is the simple desire that offenders get what they deserve. An illustration is the "eye for an eye" calculations, which prescribe exactly which punishment fits each sin (Exod 21:23–25). This "law of retaliation establishes the principle that the offender should suffer the same injury as the victim."[6] The aim of this retributive justice

---

5. Regehr, 50.
6. Regehr, 57.

is to ensure balance in justice; in other words, only an eye for an eye, not two eyes for an eye, which creates a separation between the balance of justice and the raw emotion of revenge. Many practitioners of restorative justice reject this aspect of biblical justice because they view punishment/retribution as something contrary to justice. Therefore, even though restorative justice is in many ways grounded in the biblical concept, this important aspect is sometimes ignored. We must be prepared to bear the consequences of our actions, and although our modern (or postmodern) sensibilities make it difficult to accept the idea of punishment and retribution, it is an important concept in the Bible. It is also important to note that in most biblical passages where God's actions are on behalf of retributive justice, "God takes up the cause of the one who has suffered, and rebalances the moral universe"[7] – i.e. there is evil in the world and it must be confronted.

Justice as Judgment

A possible translation for the word *mishpat* is "judgment," and as we have already seen, *mishpat* can also be justice, so that both concepts are closely linked. Judgment "is an act of God for the oppressed and against those who oppress. God executes judgment in order to call Israel to return, so that *mishpat* as judgment is the precursor to repentance. . . . In this sense, judgment is also an act of hope."[8] It is significant that there is hope, and judgment is directed toward the future. In Isaiah 19, we see that God passes judgment on Egypt because of its sin. In response to God's judgment and punishment, Egypt cries out to God for rescue, and the Lord hears its cries. We see in this passage that "God both strikes and heals, and strikes in order to heal."[9] Judgment brings our sin to the surface so we are forced to acknowledge it, and then we are given a choice: to continue in our sin or to change and accept God's healing. The fact that we are faced with a choice means that we have agency and that we control our own destiny to a certain extent. This does not mean, however, "that choices are completely unconstrained. Choices are subject to a wide variety of social, economic, and psychological constraints, as well as the constraint of divine will."[10] While constraints should be taken into account, we are still responsible for our actions. In the Bible, the exodus narrative clearly shows that Egypt was

---

7. Regehr, 59.
8. Regehr, 59–60.
9. Regehr, 60.
10. Regehr, 61.

judged by God, and the children of Israel were liberated. But God also used this liberation to hold the children of Israel accountable, commanding that they remember their bondage in Egypt, that they remember that God had freed them. Therefore, they are to treat the alien, the poor, the widow, and the orphan with justice.

Justice as Mercy

If we only consider the above aspects of justice – retribution, vengeance, punishment, and judgment – then the biblical view of justice seems familiar. However, in Psalm 85:10 we see something new. In this verse, mercy and truth meet, justice and peace kiss. This is different from the traditional view, for here justice is joined with mercy. And while this mercy extends to the guilty, who we may believe do not deserve it, it does not exclude punishment for them: "God does not declare the guilty innocent or the innocent guilty, or say it really doesn't matter. There is no such thing as mercy unless right is right and wrong is wrong."[11] This leads us to forgiveness. Although God forgives, "Mercy is not something that can be claimed, as if the standards were faulty or impossibly high, and God really owes us leniency. Mercy finds us condemned, and then for some reason we do not know, set free."[12] Justice as mercy is seen in the New Testament in the parable of the Prodigal Son. The son returns home having sinned, and expects to be punished and judged, but is instead met with justice as mercy – "a justice that returns the son to the covenant community of the family, an extravagant justice that comes as a surprise, and yet is completely in keeping with the character of the father who is clearly awaiting the return of his son."[13]

Justice as Forgiveness

In the Bible, two Hebrew words are used for forgiveness: *nasa* and *salach*. *Nasa* means "to lift" in a literal and figurative sense – to take away the sin and guilt. In Psalm 103:3, God is described "as one who forgives (*salach*) all your iniquities, who heals all your diseases, linking forgiveness with healing."[14] This link between forgiveness and healing is seen in the New Testament when Jesus

---

11. Gowan, *Theology in Exodus*, 237.
12. Gowan, 237.
13. Regehr, "Justice and Forgiveness," 68.
14. Regehr, 69–70.

heals and forgives the lame man in Mark 2:1–12. Forgiveness is also linked to cleansing in Jeremiah 33:8, when God declares, "I will cleanse them from all the sins they have committed against me, and will forgive all their sins of rebellion against me." In Isaiah 33, we see a presentation of *shalom*, or peace, and we see that God promises to heal all illness and forgive all sin. This indicates that forgiveness is linked to *shalom*, and we have already seen that *shalom* is linked to *tsedeq*, or justice. Therefore, forgiveness is strongly linked to justice. We see this in the parable of the Unmerciful Servant in Matthew 18:23–35, where the slave whose huge debt was forgiven did not have mercy on his fellow slave who owed him a small debt. This parable "connects forgiveness with the cancellation of financial obligation, divine forgiveness, and the obligations of human forgiveness."[15] The forgiveness and mercy we receive from God is dependent on our ability to forgive and show mercy to others. It is clear that as followers of Christ the Messiah, we are commanded to forgive – from Jesus's Sermon on the Mount to his claim that we are to forgive seventy times seven. It is also clear that to achieve justice and peace, forgiveness must be present.

Justice as Reconciliation

In the Old Testament, reconciliation is presented as the "ending of punishment and the restoration of Israel to living in conditions of *shalom*, the restoration of the covenant."[16] The cycle of sin, judgment, a call to repentance, punishment, and finally a return to *shalom* – and ultimately reconciliation – is found in the narrative of Hosea. At the conclusion of Hosea, we are presented with an image of "God's people as a fragrant garden, a blossoming vine, living in the shadow of God."[17] This is the restoration of the relationship between God and his children. In the New Testament, reconciliation becomes a central component of Christian theology. The reconciliation is both vertical (between us and God) and horizontal (between us and our fellow humans): "God was reconciling the world to himself in Christ" (2 Cor 5:19) and "he himself is our peace, who has made the two groups one and has destroyed the barrier, the dividing wall of hostility" (Eph 2:14). For true justice to be done, reconciliation must occur, for

> genuine justice, the justice that makes things better, is never satisfied merely by following rules, however equitable they are,

---

15. Regehr, 71.
16. Regehr, 74.
17. Regehr, 74.

or by asserting legal rights, however fair that may be. It is satisfied only when relationships are restored and the destructive power of evil is defeated, and this requires a freely chosen relinquishment of the logic of – and legal right to – an eye for an eye and a tooth for a tooth.[18]

Justice is not just upholding the law, but the restoration of relationships and the defeat of evil, which is only possible through reconciliation.

Justice as Repentance

In the Old Testament, repentance is presented as turning (*shub*). Thus, the call for repentance is a call to turn away from sin, injustice, and evil, and to turn toward God and justice. In Jeremiah, we see God speaking as a father spurned by his son, or a husband spurned by his wife. The children of Israel, in spurning God, have also spurned their inheritance.[19] Eventually, the child realizes that she/he has forgotten God and turned away from righteousness. "In response, God again invites the faithless, the turned away ones, to return, and to redirect themselves toward God."[20] The call for repentance is also an implicit discussion of what the faithless child or wife is turning from and what they are turning toward. As we have already seen in our discussion of *tsedeq*, *shalom*, and *mishpat*, "a significant aspect of God's doing justice is the bringing of punishment on Israel for its failure to practice *tsedeq*, to live *shalom*. By implication, the turning to God would mean a new practice of living *tsedeq* and *shalom*."[21] Therefore, repentance is not only turning away from evil but turning toward justice.

Justice in the New Testament

The Greek word for justice used in the New Testament is *dikaios*, which appears more than two hundred times. Like the Hebrew words for justice, it is connected to the concept of righteousness. Unfortunately, in many translations the word *dikaios* is translated as righteousness and not justice. "Of the two hundred times that *dikaios* is used in Scripture, most versions only use the

---

18. Boadt, *Jeremiah 1-25*, 33.
19. Brueggemann, *Commentary of Jeremiah*, 47.
20. Regehr, "Justice and Forgiveness," 77.
21. Regehr, 78.

translation *justice* once (Col 4:1)."[22] This has led to the false idea that the New Testament is not concerned with justice, especially among evangelicals. The evangelical church "has emphasized personal righteousness and piety and has missed much of the intended meaning bursting through the Scriptures about justice. It is critical to understand that righteousness and justice are interconnected in both Testaments."[23]

Whereas the Old Testament focuses on righteousness and justice through obedience to the law, the New Testament is more concerned with righteousness and justice through faith in the Messiah, repenting from sin, and living justly.

In the gospels, Jesus constantly challenged the religious authorities (the Pharisees) and political authorities (the Romans) about injustice. He continually challenged the dominant social hierarchy of the time, healing, and casting out demons on the Sabbath, and associating with women, fishermen, Samaritans, tax collectors, and prostitutes. Jesus's self-proclaimed mission – in coming to save offenders and elevating children above the religious Pharisees – was to serve the sinners and not the righteous. The statement "so the last will be first and the first will be last" (Matt 20:16) is a good way to summarize much of what Jesus hoped to accomplish while on earth.

In addressing the prostitute in Luke 7, Jesus recognizes that the moral failings and social injustices within society are inextricably linked to theology. As Jesus pronounces the woman forgiven, the implication is that she will sin no more and leave her old life of prostitution behind. Jesus's "restorative" justice, therefore, addresses both the person and the political and economic situation in which he or she is to be found.[24] He destabilizes the existing social order of the time and vindicates the sinner by situating them in the appropriate position in society.

It is Christ's activity on the cross which finally deals with the debt of sin which not only corrupts the personal and individual but distorts the social and created order of the world. This is because the cross represents God's mercy and grace, an element of justice which is counter to our modern conception of impartial, objective justice. In fact, there "is a profound 'injustice' about the God of the biblical tradition. It is called *grace*."[25]

The parable of the Prodigal Son in Luke 15:11–32 contains an example of this grace. There is something "unjust" about the way the prodigal son is

---

22. Cannon, *Social Justice Handbook*, 21.
23. Cannon, 21.
24. Myers and Enns, *Ambassadors of Reconciliation*.
25. Volf, *Exclusion and Embrace*, 221.

welcomed home by his father and rewarded even more than the son who was faithful. How can this be? "Why does God not treat all people equally but attends to each person in their specificity? Why does God not abstract from the relationship but instead lets the relationship shape judgments and actions?"[26] Because to do so would not be true justice. Absolute justice is possible only when the individual case is taken into account. The attempt to achieve absolute justice often creates further injustices. People are unique and cannot be judged in the same way. To attain true justice, we must assess what is appropriate in each particular situation, which "cannot be adequately done . . . if no love is in play. Without the will to embrace, justice is likely to be unjust."[27] Without love for one another, especially for those who have wronged us, we can never have real justice. This love is only possible in the context of God's sacrifice on the cross.

Application of Biblical Justice

God's concern with justice, with *tsedeq*, applies to all people in the Old Testament. For example, in Amos 1:11 God warns of his wrath against Edom because of its injustice. The punishment Edom is to suffer is the same as the punishment that the children of Israel are to receive for their injustice in Amos 2:6–8. The children of Israel failed to be an example of justice to the surrounding nations. "Israel's failure to practice justice destroys the hope of the nations. Israel's faithfulness is for the sake of the nations, that they might see the light of God's justice and love. When Israel is unfaithful, there is no light to be seen."[28] This clearly indicates that biblical justice has universal application and is intended for everyone, not just the children of Israel.

The goal was always to bring justice to all the nations through the story and example of the children of Israel. The suffering servant in Isaiah 53, whom the followers of Jesus have identified as the Messiah, suffered because of his attempt to bring about justice. Therefore, it is the task of all believers in the Messiah to work toward biblical justice.

While the criminal justice system and all modern theories of justice have been influenced by the concepts of biblical justice, most have embraced only some of its aspects. The criminal justice system (which emphasizes retribution/repayment) and the theorists of restorative justice are two examples. Theorists

---

26. Volf, 222.
27. Volf, 224.
28. Grimsrud, "Healing Justice," 76.

of restorative justice, in response to what they view as the failed criminal justice system, struggle to accept the ideas of judgment and punishment. This is problematic, for to fully understand and apply the principles of biblical justice, all the inter-connected elements should be accepted.

Judgment has been defined as "an act of moral discrimination that pronounces upon a preceding act or existing state of affairs to establish a new public context."[29] This definition can be broken down into three parts: judgment is an act of moral discrimination that divides right from wrong; it is reactive in that it speaks to a past act or existing state of affairs; and it creates a context for future action.[30]

This means that judgment makes a clear demarcation between right and wrong. Without judgment, there can be no distinction between good and evil and therefore no basis for justice. Judgment presumes that doing wrong is a choice, but as we have seen, judgment should also recall that this choice is made under specific constraints and circumstances which must be taken into account.

> Judgment has to be clear about what is judged and what is not, so that offenders take responsibility for the choices they make, while not being held responsible for the social forces that played a role in these choices. Issues of social class, family origin, education, mental health, racist social structures, and much more play a role in the choices offenders make.[31]

Still, once the choice is made, the offender must take responsibility for it and for its consequences.

Once judgment is rendered, there is a possibility of change in the future. The offender must understand that what he/she did was wrong, and experience guilt and remorse, but this is not enough. The offender must also change his/her behavior, so that the injustice will end. Once this has occurred, the offender may learn to act against injustice and work toward the establishment of justice. This experience of judgment is not a death sentence; it allows for a positive change to occur. "The experience of judgment that produces change in the offender enables the offender to participate in the task of helping others to

---

29. O'Donovan, *Ways of Judgment*, 7.
30. Regehr, "Justice and Forgiveness," 85.
31. Regehr, 87.

make the same change, to assist in the undoing of harms caused by others in similar circumstances."[32]

Repayment is another concept which is central to biblical justice but has mostly been ignored by modern theories of restorative justice. Most theorists of restorative justice focus on encouraging dialogue between the offender and the offended and helping the offender to undo the harm caused. Restorative justice does not reflect what is expressed in the Bible, such as the verse in Isaiah, "According to what they have done, so will he repay wrath to his enemies and retribution to his foes" (Isa 59:18). Restorative justice has "specifically framed itself in a way that excludes vindication, vengeance, retribution, and punishment."[33]

Writers on restorative justice tend to skirt the issues of repayment and punishment or postulate an opposition between judgment and mercy, favoring mercy. Similarly, the criminal justice system leaves no room for mercy and forgiveness and leans heavily on the side of punishment. Biblical justice, however, does not separate judgment and mercy, and does not divide punishment and forgiveness, but holds them all in balance. It is restorative justice in a very real sense because the aim of God's justice is to restore justice and peace based on his covenant with humankind. His justice is "saving justice where punishment of the sinner is an integral part of restoration. . . . God's justice is a restorative or reconstructive justice before it is a punitive or destructive justice."[34]

We cannot do away with the retributive or punitive aspects of justice, for if we do, we blur the lines between right and wrong. Judgment and punishment are crucial to justice. But we must remember that God's plan for justice is to reconcile and restore. He does not punish for the sake of punishment, but to save those who have sinned and caused injustice, and for the sake of his covenant.

---

32. Regehr, 90.
33. Regehr, 93.
34. Marshall, *Beyond Retribution*, 137.

Stage Six

Taking Steps

25

Christian Perspectives on Change: Personal and Societal Change

By Mae Elise Cannon

Therefore, I urge you, brothers and sisters, in view of God's mercy, to offer your bodies as a living sacrifice, holy and pleasing to God – this is your true and proper worship. Do not conform to the pattern of this world, but be transformed by the renewing of your mind. Then you will be able to test and approve what God's will is – his good, pleasing and perfect will. (Rom 12:1–2)

Transformation is the process of radical change. As Christians, we believe the process of personal transformation happens because of the presence of the Holy Spirit and the transforming power of God in our lives. Individuals must willingly submit and engage in this process of change as God performs the work of shaping, molding, and changing his followers more into his image and likeness. Change is an exciting and complex process. Personal change happens when someone makes an intentional decision to depend on God and allow the transforming power of the Holy Spirit into one's life. Change, however, does not only occur on a personal level. Every individual is part of a community or larger system. One's intimate community begins with those in one's immediate circle of family and close friends, yet when an individual experiences personal transformation and change, the entire system is affected. As one person changes behaviors, thoughts, ideas, and actions, others in relationship with that individual also experience change. Family, friends, and the larger community must then choose how to respond to the changes they experience and observe in the transformed individual. Thus, as each of us pursues the ongoing process of transformation into the likeness of Christ, we also have the ability to influence and provoke change within our immediate and extensive relationships in the larger community. What great hope this provides. God promises that he will complete the work of transformation that he has begun in us that we might be confident: "He who began a good work in you will carry it on to completion until the day of Christ Jesus" (Phil 1:6). However, our personal transformation is not only for our own benefit: "For it is God who works in you to will and to act in order to fulfill his good purpose" (Phil 2:13). We are transformed so that we might better fulfill the purposes that God has ordained for us. It is a great privilege to know that not only does God desire for us to experience personal change but he also desires us to be agents of change in the world.

Personal Transformation and Individual Change

Personal change begins by the process of submitting oneself to God. This occurs most directly in a posture of repentance. When someone realizes the ways that he or she has not honored God, and has failed to fulfill his creeds and commandments, there are many possible responses. The response that is desired by God is one of repentance; recognition of sin, calling for forgiveness and commitment to God's authority[1] Henry Cloud and John Townsend, two Christian psychologists, write: "Repentance, simply put, is a change in direction. It is a movement away from the destructive path back toward God's ways."[2] As we enter the process of repentance, we place ourselves in a position to be transformed by the Holy Spirit so that our ways might become more like the thoughts, beliefs, and actions desired by God. As we acknowledge and recognize the errors of our ways and submit to God in an attitude of repentance, individual change and personal transformation occur.

One of my favorite books about the process of personal change is by Henry Cloud and John Townsend called *How People Grow: What the Bible Reveals about Personal Growth*. Cloud and Townsend walk their readers through the process of spiritual growth and personal transformation. One of their reminders is the critical part that love plays in the process of change. Love compels change. Cloud and Townsend write, "When we realize we are hurting

---

1. Corrie, *Dictionary of Mission Theology*, 336.
2. Cloud and Townsend, *How People Grow*, 288.

someone we love, we change. Love and empathy change us. We treat others as we would want to be treated. Love constrains us."[3] When we know we are loved, we feel safe and are more willing to be vulnerable. One of the first conditions for growth and change is to know that we are secure, both in our relationship with God and in our relationships with others.[4] The security of knowing we are loved allows us to experience personal transformation and be better able to love others.

Individual change and transformations in personal relationships are not the only types of change expected from the people of God. As the body of Christ, when an individual experiences personal transformation, the entire community is influenced as a result of this change. We are told in 1 Corinthians 12:24–26 that we are each a part of the body of Christ: "But God has put the body together, giving greater honor to the parts that lacked it, so that there should be no division in the body, but that its parts should have equal concern for each other. If one part suffers, every part suffers with it; if one part is honored, every part rejoices with it." When one person in the body experiences transformation and change, the entire body is affected. Just as when one person is celebrated, the entire body experiences joy. Similarly, if one part of the body suffers, the larger community suffers also. Personal transformation does not happen in isolation, but directly correlates with the direction and progression of one's immediate community and larger society. In fact, Christians are called to intentionally play a part in bringing about societal change and transformation as a means of fulfilling God's purposes for the world.

Sociocultural Transformation and Change in Society

Charles Kraft writes in *Anthropology for Christian Witness*, "All change in culture is initiated in the minds of the people who live in that culture."[5] This should be greatly encouraging news as it implies that individuals can provoke change and shape the future direction of their cultures and society. Kraft further suggests that "all sociocultural change starts with changes in the minds of individuals. The starting point for change is a new perspective. We can thus change our habitual use of cultural structures to enable us to serve God, rather than the ends ordinarily recommended by the society of which we are a part."[6]

---

3. Cloud and Townsend, 172.
4. Cloud and Townsend, 96.
5. Kraft, *Anthropology for Christian Witness*, 366.
6. Kraft, 359.

In other words, following the example of Jesus, Christians have the opportunity to use cultural structures in a different way. Rather than "conforming to the patterns of this world" (Rom 12:1–2), we are given the opportunity to have a new perspective, due to the transformation of our minds, which allows us to engage with our society differently. As our paradigms and perspectives shift and change, we are better equipped to be agents of change who use the systems and structures of society to better serve God. Kraft asserts, "The Gospel always results in changes – changes in people who initially change the way they use their culture and may then go on to alter the structures themselves to become more adequate vehicles for God's working."[7] It is a great privilege and responsibility to bring about change in the world. This responsibility should be taken seriously so that Christians may passionately pursue righteousness, justice, and other societal attributes that are close to the heart of God.

God's Desire for Community Change

Much could be said about the personal transformation and change which are critical components of personal discipleship and a growing relationship with Christ. However, the remainder of this section focuses on the process of bringing about societal change and transformation within community. Far too often the church focuses on the process of individual transformation and neglects to address God's call to his community to be an agent of change in the world. As we look more deeply at the question of societal change, it is important to seek to understand God's desire. Throughout the New Testament, Jesus's teaching addresses the question of which role people should play in their society. Jesus came to the earth so that the good news of the kingdom of God might be preached (Luke 16:16). The disciples were similarly instructed to go out, to heal the sick, and to preach the good news of the kingdom of God (Luke 9:2). Similarly, today, we are instructed to go into the world making disciples of all nations (Matt 28:19) and to respond to the needs of the least of these (Matt 25:40). Believers are instructed to pursue personal righteousness and right relationship with God, while also being witnesses of the good news of the gospel, sharing the message of salvation in Jesus Christ, and working to right the wrongs in society. How do these changes occur, what steps might be taken to achieve them, and what might be the barriers to effective change?

---

7. Kraft, 360.

Barriers to Change

People do not like to change, and "since people tend to be quite protective of their worldview assumptions, these provide the primary barriers to change,"[8] writes Kraft. Acknowledging that "people can be quite protective of their worldview assumptions" is an important starting point. Thus, it is important to invite people to discover their underlying assumptions and then to gently enter into the process of challenging them. Kraft reminds his readers that people are often the greatest inhibitors to effective change: "Worldview does not block change; it is the people following the guidelines of the worldview who throw up the barriers. It is people who will emote, think, interpret, evaluate, make commitments, explain, relate, and adapt on the basis either of traditional assumptions or changed assumptions, and people tend to do this habitually, without thinking."[9] Although the process can be difficult and conflict ridden, if individuals and communities are going to change, their inherent assumptions about the world must be brought to the surface.

If people hold so tightly to their inherent assumptions of the world, how can change occur? Many change agents act out of a feeling of need because they have experienced some kind of deprivation, dissatisfaction, or disaffection. While not experiencing the deprivation personally, individuals may have a personal and deep connection to other individuals or communities who suffer deprivation. Individuals who provoke change often exhibit an openness to change through expressed and overt interest, curiosity, or inclination to experiment.[10] In addition, Kraft argues that freedom is a necessary condition in the pursuit of change. In environments of freedom, individuals have more room to be creative and to dream, which contribute to the belief that change is possible. Kraft argues that when freedom is inhibited, there is less room for people to discover the necessity for change because "all one's time and energy is expended in merely surviving [and] creativity tends to be squelched."[11] The belief in possibility and the advisability of change is necessary for people to hope that change is possible. Human motivations also inspire change as people desire an increase in "personal standing" and are motivated by the desire for "meaningfulness, economic gain, prestige, and power, whether spiritual or

---

8. Kraft, 381.
9. Kraft, 385.
10. Kraft, 392.
11. Kraft, 392.

social."[12] Thus, people both initiate and provoke change and also inhibit and obstruct it.

Practical Inhibitors to Change

John Kotter wrote an excellent book for Harvard Business School titled *Leading Change*, about how one can develop an action plan to bring about change within organizations. He includes several challenges to change which relate to societal change as well.[13]

First on his list is complacency. He writes that the quest for change – and movement into new and unknown territory – must first be inspired by passion and urgency in order to overcome the negative force of complacency.

His second deterrent to change is the absence of a powerful team of committed individuals to guide and implement it, while the third challenge derives from "underestimating the power of vision."[14] As the Bible says, "Without a vision, the people will perish" (Prov 29:18). Cloud and Townsend write, "If we are to deeply help people on the path to spiritual growth, we have to know where we come from, where we went from there, and where we are heading."[15]

The fourth inhibitor is under-communication of vision. A group, community, or organization may have the greatest vision in the world; but if no one knows about it, they won't be inspired and encouraged to work toward it. Kotter says that leaders have a tendency to under-communicate vision by a factor of 10, 100, or even 1,000.[16]

The fifth barrier to effective change is obstacles which block vision. For example, Kraft mentions that "freedom" is a necessary component for creative space in which people can dream about ways that change might occur. While I agree, the lack of freedom must not become a roadblock which prevents change. Consider the social justice and reform movements around the world such as the civil rights movement in the United States and the anti-apartheid movement in South Africa. In both cases the vision for liberty, justice, and human rights was greater than the lack of political freedom. Obstacles must not be allowed to block the vision.

---

12. Kraft, 392.
13. The following challenges to change are taken from Kotter, *Leading Change*, 16.
14. Kotter, 16.
15. Cloud and Townsend, *How People Grow*, 26.
16. Kotter, *Leading Change*, 16.

The sixth important point is that short-term wins should always be celebrated. There will inevitably be challenges and roadblocks on the road to effective change, which may be discouraging and even immobilizing, so it is important to counterbalance them by celebrating small wins and short-term steps in the right direction. When the sought-after change requires huge transformation, the process may seem overwhelming and the goal unobtainable. The achievement of reasonable short-term goals facilitates a sense that progress is being made toward realizing the vision, and acknowledging these small successes keeps people motivated.

Just as celebrating small-scale victories is important, his seventh point is that it is critical not to declare victory prematurely or to mistake small-scale victories for attainment of the desired goal. Change must be deeply ingrained in a culture to ensure that regression does not occur, and this may take years.[17] According to Kotter, a "premature victory celebration stops all of the momentum."[18]

The eighth and final inhibitor to lasting change is the failure to anchor change into one's lifestyle and culture. As Kraft mentions, truly effective change shifts people's worldview and provides a different perspective about the way things are and should be. Once change is anchored within a community and society, it is helpful for people to understand how their changes in behavior and actions have helped bring about the desired change. True change leads to shifts in culture as the larger community embodies the desired change.

Process of Change

The process of ongoing change is hard work. People will pursue change if they hope and believe that things can be different. If individuals and communities are overcome by hopelessness, they will be hard-pressed to take intentional action to bring about change. As the above theological reflection suggests, God plays a significant part in the transformation process. We can take intentional actions to put ourselves in positions where change can occur, but God functions as the change agent within us. Then, because of God's work within us, humans receive the opportunity to be agents of change in the world.

The following approach briefly presents a further eight components related to the process of change, which have been adapted to formulate a more holistic approach to change within communities.

---

17. Kotter, 13.
18. Kotter, 13.

Step 1: Identifying the Problem

To pursue intentional change, one must have a clear idea of the problem being addressed. Often people feel that "something isn't right" but lack a clear sense of what the problem might be. It is important to break down the problems into their component parts and to address the specifics to clarify assumptions and differences of opinion.

Step 2: Overcoming Complacency

Cloud and Townsend write: "Do not wait for change to happen. Take the initiative to face what you have been afraid to know."[19] Overcoming complacency means willingness to face the reality of existing problems. To achieve this one must willingly enter into the process of awareness and step outside personal paradigms to view the world from a larger perspective. With regard to the Israeli-Palestinian conflict, the process of problem identification and overcoming complacency can take a great deal of time, energy, and resources. When group assumptions and paradigms are so different from each other, it is inevitable that the search for common ground will require time and effort. However, the Bible promises that with God nothing is impossible.

Step 3: Developing a Dynamic Team

"For just as each of us has one body with many members, and these members do not all have the same function, so in Christ we, though many, form one body, and each member belongs to all the others" (Rom 12:3–5). I have taught entire workshops about developing a dynamic team, so this short paragraph is a woefully inadequate description. That said, developing a dynamic leadership team is critical to practicing biblical community in any setting. Regardless of whether the group is comprised of Christians or those from other faiths, a leadership team will help set the course and direction for the occurrence of change. Ultimately, a group of people with unique gifts and collective resources can accomplish more through their collaborative efforts than they could alone. An effective leadership team is vital for stimulating growth and change within a community.

---

19. Cloud and Townsend, *How People Grow*, 340.

Step 4: Defining Reality

One of my leadership mentors was mentored by corporate executive and leadership guru Max Dupree. Dupree is known for his book *The Art of Leadership* and has taught workshops and courses across the United States. I have great appreciation for what I have learned from Max's writings and through his direct influence on my leadership mentor. One adage credited to Dupree is "The first task of a leader is to define reality." Once a leadership team has been established, the next step is to have a clear and (as much as possible) unbiased perspective about the reality of the current situation. While I believe this to be true, I would argue that defining reality is actually a leader's second task.

Several years ago, I managed a team of about twenty people at a medium-sized church. I was excited about my mission to help them become more effective and purposeful and, ultimately, to bring about change within the church community. I took to heart the principle that "The first task of a leader is to define reality." One of the first meetings that I attended was with the entire staff. They had gathered for perhaps three to four hours (it felt like fifty!) to discuss the church schedule and which meetings would occur in which rooms. The meeting was long, excruciatingly detailed, and terribly boring. I thought about how much the church was spending on the salaries of all those in attendance. The meeting was an ineffective use of time. When one of the other pastors asked me what I thought, in the spirit of "defining reality," I responded: "That was the worst meeting I have ever attended. It was terribly boring and a waste of our time. Shoot me in the head." Granted, I exaggerated (only slightly) for dramatic effect. Nonetheless, the expression on this man's face made it clear that he was devastated by my comments, and I learned a very important lesson that day. The first task of a leader is to love your people. Once they know they are loved, they will be open to the process of defining reality. But first be sure they know they are loved.

In business, as in any situation, an effective way to define reality is to conduct a SWOT (strengths, weaknesses, opportunities, and threats) analysis. Strengths and weaknesses apply to internal forces which either work in your favor or challenge your objective. Opportunities and threats refer to external sources and influences. For example, government restrictions or laws may be considered external threats whereas your leadership team's talents and gifts may be internal strengths.

Step 5: Determine the Vision and Strategies for a Solution

The vision creates a picture of how the problem being addressed could be resolved and how things would look if you succeeded. A vision should be specific and clear. Once the vision is realized, the job of your group or organization will be complete. Vision sets the direction for change and motivates people to take action.[20] Vision also helps to coordinate the actions of individuals in a "remarkably fast and efficient way."[21] It is important to remember that a vision is never created in a single meeting but is a process of months or years. Once a vision has been clearly established, strategies are needed, and by this point, significant work should have been done to define the problem and determine the major resources and challenges. The process of strategic planning determines how to bring about the desired change. For example, a group whose vision is reconciliation between Christians and Muslims would determine specific strategies to move the groups and communities in that direction. While "reconciliation between Christians and Muslims" is a broad and generic vision, reconciliation between the leaders of the Christian and Muslim community in the city of Bethlehem is much more specific. Strategies might include raising awareness, building relationships, networking, and providing avenues for acceptance.

Step 6: Commit to Specific Goals

Goals are the specific outcomes that a group commits to achieving by employing the agreed-upon strategies. A goal defines the desired result a person, group, or system envisions, plans, and makes a commitment to achieve. A goal is a desired endpoint along the road to accomplishing a group's vision. Group goals must be agreed upon and must directly fulfill the common strategic purposes.

One set of criteria for developing effective goals is called SMART (specific, measurable, attainable, realistic, and timely). Often goals are not accomplished because they are not specific. A goal should be clearly measurable, attainable, and realistic. It may be challenging and difficult to achieve, but it must be possible. A goal should also have a clearly defined date and time for accomplishment.

Step 7: Celebrate Small Victories along the Way

Most change occurs gradually. Thus, it is important to have markers so a group is aware of progress being made, and an effective marker is the celebration of

---

20. Kotter, *Leading Change*, 68.
21. Kotter, 68.

small victories. Some groups may want to celebrate periodically by sharing a meal. Others may want to throw a party or hold an event. Still others may choose to honor their accomplishments creatively, by writing a song or performing a play. With ministry teams, I often encourage groups to consider the possibility of keeping a "victory journal" or log where they record and celebrate their accomplishments. The group then reviews the journal periodically to be reminded of what it has accomplished.

Step 8: Long-Term and Results-Oriented Change in Communities

Substantial change usually takes place over long periods and after significant effort. Nonetheless, change can and does occur. Once a group or community has progressed toward long-term change, the attributes, behaviors, thoughts, and perspectives related to the desired change should become deeply integrated into the culture of the community. Since "bad habits die hard," the leadership team must regularly remind the group of its common vision and purpose. Each of us plays a part in bringing about change. Some, like Paul, plant the seeds, while others, like Apollo, water the seeds once they have been planted. Ultimately it is God who makes it grow.[22] God brings about the desired change within individuals and within the world. May we willingly and intentionally embrace the process of change as we submit to the work of God in our lives and the world.

---

22. 1 Corinthians 3:5–9.

26

From Arm-Wrestling to Shaking Hands

By Salim J. Munayer

Travelling and speaking widely as I do, I see more and more that churches are divided. Congregants seem split along emotionally charged lines regarding the Israeli-Palestinian conflict. Two main, hotly debated, topics tend to emerge, in the form of questions, charges, and accusations: the historical account of the conflict and its theological implications. Often, these are intertwined. I focus here on the theological aspect, which has the most direct importance for believers both in the land and abroad. Generally speaking, most Christians can be divided into two theological camps: the Christian Zionist camp, which adheres to one form or other of dispensational theology and is usually represented by members of evangelical churches, and the social justice camp, comprised mostly of Protestant mainstream church members. Both positions can be found worldwide, and in Israel/Palestine they are closely reflected in the Israeli Messianic Jewish community and the community of Palestinian Christians, many of whom adhere to Palestinian liberation theology. Both sides have positive contributions to make to the discussion, but when the goal is reconciliation, both also present challenges.

For the community of believers in the Messiah in Israel/Palestine, the two most dominant and divisive issues are prophecy and justice. Unfortunately, it is impossible to explore the full range of opinions and theological positions in both these communities. However, even a general overview will allow for a better understanding of the current situation and, hopefully, help us to move forward. These issues, while substantial, may be overcome.

Prophecy

The theme of prophecy fulfillment and eschatology is especially important to the Israeli Messianic Jewish community, since, for many of its members, the restoration of the Jews to Eretz Yisrael is both the fulfillment of prophecy and significant for God's plan for the future. One of the most frequently quoted biblical passages attesting to this is from Ezekiel 37:1–14, where the prophet Ezekiel has his vision of dry bones into which God breathes life. For many in this community, these dry, dead bones represent the Jewish people scattered throughout the world in the Diaspora, suffering persecution and discrimination that culminated in the Holocaust. But from the depths of this suffering, God delivered his people and brought them back to the land he promised to them.

Israeli Messianic Jews and Christian Zionists make assumptions which lead them to perceive the physical restoration of Israel in the promised land, and the establishment of the modern State of Israel, as the fulfillment of this prophecy. These assumptions are usually accompanied by a belief that, through the establishment of the State of Israel, other prophecies concerning the end times will also be fulfilled. The assumptions are as follows:

1. Biblical Israel and modern Israel are one and the same, and the covenant God made with biblical Israel is still in effect, and applies to the modern State of Israel.

2. The borders of the promised land remain the same, from the time they were described in the Bible until today.

3. Prophecy is important and relates to events happening today.

4. All Christians are commanded by Scripture to bless Israel, based on Genesis 12:3.

5. The church has not replaced Israel, and the New Testament in no way cancels out the importance of the Old Testament.

6. God is not finished with the Jewish people and still has an important role for them in his redemptive plan for the entire world.

This theological perspective embodies positive elements. It allows us to feel the urgency of eschatological matters and to view God as the mover of history, whereas, in many circles, he has been relegated to personal matters. In this view, God is not only involved in our lives but also in history and the great events that shape our lives. This view has also returned the Jewish people and the role they play in Scripture and revelation to the consciousness of Christianity, challenging much of the centuries-old anti-Semitism that was present in some of the supersessionist[1] theologies. It is a perspective which makes sense, given the historical experience of the Jewish people.

However, due to the particular interpretation of history and prophecy espoused by some Israeli Messianic Jews and Christian Zionists, many of their political conclusions are dubious at best and verge on racism at worst. This is due to their emphasis on the principles of election and God's sovereignty – to the point of ignoring other aspects of God's nature. Particular interpretations of these concepts can easily lead to dehumanization and a dangerous ends-justify-the-means logic. Since God's promises must be fulfilled, anyone who stands in the way may come to be seen as merely an obstacle, an enemy of God, rather than a person.

As the Messianic Jewish leader Daniel Juster writes, "justice is the order of righteousness whereby individuals and peoples can fulfil their God intended destinies."[2] With this type of reasoning, biblical justice is seen in opposition to "unbiblical humanistic justice,"[3] which does not take into account the bigger picture of God's plan. Juster writes that biblical justice begins with God's declared will for Israel and the nations. He says that if the Jewish people do not submit to the law of God and are instead a lawless people, or if they replace God's law with human laws which contradict that law, they will find themselves suffering and resisted by God himself. He continues that, according to the same thinking, "if Palestinians refuse to recognize what God says about the Jewish people and their connection to the land of Israel, the result will also be suffering. Justice, therefore, when properly understood, is the fulfillment of God's promises and God's will."[4] When it comes to the conflict between Israelis and Palestinians, God's will is clear according to Juster, and much Palestinian and Jewish suffering can be traced to a lack of willingness to submit to God's declared will on many levels.

When such strong emphasis is placed on the "chosenness" of a people as it relates to prophecy and the end times, the theological importance, as well as the human rights, of other people will recede into the background. This limits any attempt at reconciliation, because it essentially ignores the pain and suffering

---

1. Supersessionism (also referred to as replacement theology) is the idea that the church has replaced Israel in God's plan.
2. Juster, "Messianic Jew Looks at the Land Promises," 67.
3. Juster, 67.
4. Juster, 79.

of the other, and is dangerous because it may lead to justification of almost any action as long as it is seen to help further the interpretation of God's will.

Justice

On the other side of the divide we have the Palestinian Christian community, concerned primarily with the biblical theme of justice. This is due to its profound sense of injustice at what it suffered during the *Nakba* at the hands of the Zionist movement and the State of Israel – suffering which continues today through the occupation and through Israel's discriminatory practices. This appeal for justice draws inspiration from the Old Testament prophets, who advocated for social and political justice as well as spiritual renewal.

Palestinian liberation theology, developed by Naim Ateek, has led the charge, demanding justice for the Palestinian people and providing a theological, and not just political, framework for this call. This theology was inspired by the liberation theology which emerged from Latin America and has found support among many Protestant mainline churches in the West, such as the Presbyterian Church and the Episcopal Church. Palestinian liberation theology combines the need for justice (along with an acknowledgement that justice alone is not enough), a preferential option for the poor, and a Christ-centered hermeneutic.

Ateek clearly presents the need for justice and calls for an end to the Israeli occupation of the Palestinian territories and for the establishment of a Palestinian state. However, Ateek also claims that justice alone is not enough, and that it must be accompanied by mercy, grace, and forgiveness. He follows Latin American liberation theologians in their call for a preferential option for the poor, in which Christians would side with the poor and oppressed because God himself sides with them. Finally, Ateek stresses the importance of a Christ-centered hermeneutic, viewing all passages of Scripture through an understanding of Christ and his love. In this way, many passages from the Old Testament which could be (and have been) used to support Zionist policies are understood to represent an earlier stage in the development of humanity's understanding of God. If they do not cohere with what the New Testament tells us about Christ's love, then they must be viewed as incomplete and cannot be taken at face value.

This theological perspective has proved to be an unmistakably and irreplaceably positive voice in the conflict, reminding us that there is more to God's nature than a very selective interpretation of election and sovereignty – characteristics such as mercy, compassion, love, and, above all, justice. It also reminds us that we cannot presume to do God's will while simultaneously oppressing people, that our means are a reflection of our ends, and that the Palestinian people cannot be ignored.

In the context of reconciliation, there are a number of problems with Palestinian liberation theology. First among them is the fact that it is a theology turned inward, which does not address the other except to deal with their role as oppressor. This is rather general, but it is significant, for a theology which does not engage the other will not be able to reconcile the two sides.

When Liberation Theology calls for believers in Christ to love their enemies, it is admirable. This is a perfect example of following the example and commandment of Christ in a difficult situation such as a conflict. However, it should be acknowledged that this is not an easy command to follow. While loving our enemies is not impossible, it is extremely difficult, and, if we allow ourselves to separate the world into "allies" and "enemies," usually some form of hatred will show through in our actions and attitudes. We cannot and should not accept injustice; however, by focusing all our attention on our enemies, we can easily see the situation as simplistic, blinding ourselves to our own faults and our own acts of injustice. There is also a danger of stereotyping the other side – dehumanizing them by grouping people together when, in fact, there is a range of attitudes, opinions, and responses on both sides. In short, this division oversimplifies and ignores the incredible complexity of the situation, which adds to the conflict rather than contributing to reconciliation.

It is also problematic to claim that we should have a preference for the poor based on God's preference for the poor. In this context, the "poor" are those who suffer injustice. To claim that the Palestinian people are the "poor" is basically saying that God has a preference for the Palestinian people, that he has taken a side in this conflict. This is obviously a very dangerous assumption and negatively affects possibilities for reconciliation. Interestingly, it is similar to the claim by some Israeli Messianic Jews that they are God's chosen people not because of their inherent goodness but due to his faithfulness.

Another problem with determining that believers should side with the oppressed because God does so is that, especially in a conflict like the Israeli-Palestinian conflict, both sides see themselves as the victim. Who then decides who the "poor" are? If they refuse to meet the other, reconciliation is impossible.

Finally, many have objected to a hermeneutic approach to the Bible which subjugates the Old Testament to the New Testament. While it makes sense to view all of Scripture through the person of Christ, many object to Ateek's project to "de-Zionize" the Bible, which refuses to address the Jewish people. There is no place for the Jewish people in this theology (other than as oppressors), and no recognition of their historical and spiritual attachment to the land, all of which prevents reconciliation.

Conclusion

There is a problem in the context of theology which plagues both sides and makes reconciliation impossible. We allow our theological views to prevent us from having contact with those who disagree with us, and we permit our theology to be used as a political weapon. This is not to say that theology and politics can be totally separated, or that they should be. However, we must have space in our theology for others, even if we do not agree with them. Some followers of dispensational theology refuse fellowship with people who do not accept their interpretation of prophecy. It is common for followers of Palestinian liberation theology to declare they will avoid all interaction with "the oppressor" until liberation is achieved. Both sides set political and theological preconditions with respect to meeting the other, creating a zero-sum challenge: surrender your views and adopt ours, or we will have nothing to do with you. Believers from both sides have been drafted into the conflict rather than forming a bridge across the chasm of suspicion and hatred. If we are unwilling to dialogue with one another, reconciliation is impossible. We must move from arm-wrestling to handshaking.

Unfortunately, it is beyond the scope of this article to write about the theology of reconciliation, and how God commands us to make every effort to reconcile with our brothers and sisters. Suffice it to say that an exclusive focus on prophecy fulfillment and the end times, or on justice and liberation, can never be the full picture. The choice to pursue either one alone, outside the context of the cross, will lead to violence, exclusion, and rejection. Whatever our theology, we must remember God's love, and God's commandment that we love each other. Our aim should be unity through Christ's love and through the cross, as Jesus urged, praying "that [all believers] may be one, Father, just as you are in me and I am in you. May they also be in us so that the world may believe that you have sent me" (John 17:21).

27

The Cross and Reconciliation

By Salim J. Munayer

The cross has a unique role and function in the land where Jesus walked two thousand years ago. Followers of Christ in Palestine and Israel today are essentially a minority within the Jewish and Muslim majorities, and with so much of the region defined by conflict, believers in Jesus look to him as a basis for reconciliation. While Muslims and Jews reject the cross, believers who pursue reconciliation seek to fulfill Christ's prayer for unity in John 17:21, so that their testimony of unity will reflect his work of reconciliation.

The conflict between Israelis and Palestinians is multi-faceted and (seemingly) intractable. The reality is that Israelis and Palestinians have no choice but to live in close proximity in one land. Cooperation, reconciliation, and relationships are essential. While peace accords have been attempted, political solutions have failed to mend intergroup relations or to alter attitudes of hatred and prejudice which continue to undermine political agreements and fuel the cycle of violence. Both sides are characterized by pain and enmity.

There are believers in the Messiah on both sides of the conflict – whether Palestinian Arab Christians or Israeli Messianic Jews – and neither group is immune to its impact or untouched by the tide of prejudice and hostility. The gaps – including those which separate believers – continue to widen. As violence, political ideologies, and theological disparities create rifts, followers of Jesus are compelled to address these issues in the context of the cross.

Christ's act on the cross, God extending reconciliation to us, obliges us to reconcile with others. The gospel provides a resource and a framework through which to approach the other and the enemy. Through the cross, leaders and lay people from the Israeli Messianic and Palestinian Christian communities have been coming together to live the mandate for reconciliation. Through organizations like Musalaha, people face the challenge of practicing these biblical principles in the midst of conflict. Obstacles to reconciliation regularly emerge, particularly regarding conflicts of identity, the imbalance of power, the search for justice, and the presence of prejudice, hatred, and the desire for revenge. This article discusses these trends, and how the cross models a response to these challenges.

The Cross as Atonement for Sin

The cross is a central theme in reconciliation. 1 John 4:7 describes the nature of God as love, a love made apparent through Christ's act on the cross. God is love not only in his identity, but also in his act of sending his son as atonement for our sin (1 John 4:10). This basic principle is the foundation of biblical reconciliation. God loves and embraces a world that rebels against him. All of humanity is sinful and in enmity with God, yet he declares through the cross that he wants a relationship with us that is intimate and eternal. God's embrace of sinners enables us to have a relationship with him, which in turn provides a mandate for us to embrace others.

This act on the cross not only impacts us personally and individually, but also informs our relationships and attitudes toward others. Each of us belongs to various ethnic, cultural, and religious backgrounds and is influenced by the attitudes of our groups toward other groups. Tragically, the intertwining of Israeli and Palestinian histories is colored by hatred, prejudice, and division, yet the cross can affect these perceptions.

Attitudes toward the other reflect deep-seated dehumanization and demonization, which disregard its humanity. Palestinians and Israelis often view one another as the enemy and not as individuals with lives and families. Each group demonizes the other, often employing religious verses to portray the other as the instrument of the devil and beyond redemption.

The act of Christ on the cross rejects these attitudes. God's grace, just as it extends to us in our sinful state, extends to our enemies as well, for we were all once sinners and enemies of God. He could reject the human race, yet he looks upon us with love and redeems us. His act of atonement and embrace is our model and point of reference for reconciliation.

The Cross as Liberation from Roles of Victim and Oppressor

The trends of victimization and oppression are major factors in the Israeli-

Palestinian conflict. Both Israelis and Palestinians strongly perceive themselves as victims, and therefore have difficulty perceiving themselves as a threat to the other. If one is a victim, then they cannot be the victimizer. This monopoly on victimization fails to acknowledge that each side has also played the role of perpetrator and becomes a justification for violent and sinful acts.

The victim mentality can also lead to a fatalistic perspective, with both parties believing that the enemy is full of hatred, and the lust to destroy, and will never change. This justifies the use of power and pre-emptive violence for perceived self-preservation.

The cross addresses this dynamic by redefining the roles of victim and oppressor. In as much as Christ's death addresses the victim, it also deals with the oppressor. Just as God showed his love by liberating the oppressed, the oppressor is also set free in the cross and both are liberated from the cycles of conflict.

We are often mired in arguments and a vicious cycle of competing narratives and divergent perceptions of truth and justice, which leads to violence and ends in a cycle of more violence and revenge. As the cycle assumes a life of its own, people forget the origins and main issues of the conflict. The cross can help us to avoid this cycle because truth and justice is in Christ on the cross.

In the cross we see the reality of our own injustice, shortcomings, and contributions to the conflict. The cross opens the way for changing our perceptions of others and diverts us from the cycle of revenge and retaliation. "Vengeance is mine," says the Lord. He will administer retaliation and justice. It is fundamental to recognize that God, who knows and sees all, takes upon himself the role of judge. To take on the task of judgment is to assume the role and authority of God. By taking upon himself the revenge and punishment of evil, God frees us from focusing our lives on hatred and vengeance – frees us from lives that are damaging to ourselves and others. This is an important aspect of breaking the cycle of retaliation because we are freed from the bondage of thinking about the injustice. In Middle Eastern history, due to a lack of central authority, families assumed the role of administering justice, and thus vengeance became a strong cultural element. The cross brings an alternative message: God is the instrument of justice. Through the cross, we are liberated from the feelings of injustice and the mentality of a victim, and we come to recognize where we, too, deserve God's wrath and judgment.

In receiving freedom through the cross as either victim or oppressor, we can be engaged in imitating what God did for us. After being transformed, we can become part of transformative relationships. Receiving what Christ did on the cross for each of us frees both sides to engage with the other in an act of love and embrace. Through forgiveness and confession, both the oppressor and the oppressed are released, and through this freedom we can develop relationships and community.

The Cross as Solidarity with the Human Condition of Suffering

Christ, through his life, death, and resurrection, identifies with those who suffer and are oppressed. Jesus said, "The Spirit of the Lord is on me, because he has anointed me to proclaim good news to the poor. He has sent me to proclaim freedom for the prisoners and recovery of sight for the blind, to set the oppressed free, to proclaim the year of the Lord's favor" (Luke 4:18–19). Christ brings deliverance to the spiritual, social, and physical life of the victim.

Jesus's experience of suffering and his teachings concerning the sufferer compel us to attitudes of compassion, even toward our enemies. His sympathy toward the victim is not only a comfort to those who suffer, but also a demand for the same from us. In a conflict where both sides suffer from a victim mentality, they are each blind to the suffering of the other. While also being a source of redemption and relief, the cross presents a challenge to look beyond our own situation and attend to the suffering and pain of others. God is urging us to be like him, to have solidarity in suffering and bring freedom to the oppressed.

The Cross Changes and Transforms Identity

Issues of identity and group belonging are major aspects of the conflict and have significant influence on the way parties relate to one another. In our context, religion is a major defining factor of identity, separating Christian, Jew, and Muslim, and playing an important role in the interaction between the groups.

The cross not only frees us of our identities as sinners and victims or oppressors, but also grants us security in our identities. The perfect love that casts out fear (1 John 4:18) protects us from guilt, from fear of sin, and from fear of rejection, thus providing security. This is significant in a conflict comprising major struggles and insecurities concerning identity and rejection of the other.

The determination of identity can be a political statement which may affirm or deny one's existence, as the dynamic between the weak and the powerful plays its role. Often, the weak feel the need to define themselves in a way which appeases the strong for reasons of survival, prosperity, and access to power. As a result, they may deny elements of their cultural identity. This is a common struggle for the Palestinian Arab citizens of Israel. In the eyes of some, the word "Palestinian" itself is a political statement that might be threatening.

In contrast, the cross frees us to be who we are because it affirms God's love for all creation and humanity. We are created in God's image and likeness, as Arab, Jewish, Israeli, or Palestinian. The Bible assures us of God's love for all, and says, "There is neither Jew nor Gentile, neither slave nor free, nor is there male and female, for you are all one in Christ Jesus" (Gal 3:28). However, these boundaries do not cease to exist, and the characteristics of Jew and Greek or man and woman are not removed but rather transformed according to God's purposes.

We can acquire an understanding of our identity that is complementary and not contradictory to the behavior and identity of others. The cross which frees us to be ourselves also bestows the security and freedom to engage with others; and as we engage with others, just as when we encounter God, the encounter is transformative.

Some aspects of our identity require transformation. When we identify with a group, we adopt certain attitudes which confirm our sense of self and self-esteem. Many aspects of our identity are positive expressions of culture, tradition, and rich histories, but at the same time, our identification with a group can mean adopting certain negative attitudes toward the other. Social identity theory claims that the result of categorizing ourselves as a specific group is often the creation of discrimination toward those outside the group.

There is the tendency to distinguish between "us" and "them," and to relate only to one's own group favorably and with sensitivity. We understand our own group, recognize its qualities, and become attached to it. We overlook our shortcomings because it is important to distinguish between us (who are right and good and merciful) and them (who are evil and wrong).

We often fail to see plurality on the other side. We generalize and stereotype the others, declaring, "They are full of hate and want to destroy us," or "They are savages and barbarians." We are unable to see the others as individuals with unique feelings and thoughts, as God created them, and too easily dehumanize them. While we understand and perhaps accept the range of sentiment and opinion within our own group, we do not recognize the debates and disagreements within the other group. Rather, we see them as one front united against us.

Palestinians feel that all Israelis are alike and cannot be trusted, while Israelis believe the same about Palestinians. We tend to assume that the other side firmly opposes us and will never accept peace, regardless of what they may say, and find it hard to believe anything positive about them.

The cross challenges these attitudes and provides a firm alternative to these divisions: our identity is transformed as we are atoned for, redeemed, and receive new eyes through which to understand the other. The other is offered the same grace and the same transformation of identity.

Ephesians 2 is a key passage which touches on identity, intergroup attitudes, and ethnic conflict. As stated in verses 14–16, the cross created one new humanity from the two. God is not demanding that Israelis and Palestinians surrender their identity. In fact, the two groups must create a third identity, a new humanity – the new community of the people of God. Too often, group relationships contain denial and rejection of the other's identity, as one group demands that the other submit or conform to its wishes. Aspects of culture, heritage, and history are suppressed because they clash or make one side uncomfortable. In Ephesians, Paul says to bring your identity with you to the cross because it is transformed in Jesus to create a new community of the people of God, where each person contributes from the richness of his or her identity. As a result, both groups will experience peace because both are reconciled to God in one body through the cross.

The Cross Transforms Our Attitude toward the Other

In this act of reconciliation, Christ brought an end to hostility and enmity by bringing people together. There is interdependency in our reconciliation to God. We are dependent on each other to end the hostility between our groups and within ourselves. There is solidarity in sinfulness and solidarity in redemption. Our identities are transformed in relationship, not in separation. When coming to the foot of the cross, we need each other so we can deal with the hostility within our hearts and establish peace.

Ephesians 2 confronts the hostility in intergroup relationships. While addressing enmity on the personal level, this passage also deals with enmity between groups. In our case, the hatred results from the violent struggle over land. In verse 11, Paul discusses relationships between Jews and non-Jews during the days of the early church. In the days before the early church, Jews did not view non-Jews favorably, calling them names and viewing them as outsiders, and the communities were alienated. Paul declares that they came together through Jesus's sacrifice on the cross. Those "who once were far away have been brought near by the blood of Christ" (v. 13). People who did not experience God's actions and blessing in history were now embraced.

The Cross Creates a New Community

Peace comes not as a new ideology or political solution but as the result of the identity and actions of Jesus. One aspect of peace in Ephesians 2 is humanity's peace with God as a result of his forgiveness. Another aspect of peace is the end of separation or strife among groups. This peace results from people uniting through the spirit of God which cleanses us of sin and brings us to the Father. Peace in humanity is fundamentally related to humanity's peace with God.

For Israeli and Palestinian believers, this means an end to mutual hostility. We are no longer strangers and cannot desire to destroy the other group. We are now equals and belong to the same family; we are together under the judgment and grace of God. This unity diffuses the tension by adding a new aspect to our identities. God brings us together as his people in a community which embraces rather than rejects the other. We are fellow citizens (Eph 2:19).

The purpose of our unity is to build a dwelling place for the Spirit of God, and we all receive different roles to achieve it. In essence, by removing the dividing wall of hostility, the cross enables groups to move forward toward cooperation.

Our transformed identity, and belonging to a new kingdom, is liberating. Our identity is secure because we are the beloved and forgiven of God, and now we can engage. The freedom and security received in the cross through self-giving is an imitation of Christ. It removes us from the cycle of revenge because we now view oppressed and oppressors from a new perspective. There will always be different views – historical narratives will clash and theological understandings will not concur. What will change is our understanding of and attitudes toward the other. We surrender the selfish, victimized identity. Liberated, we are secure enough to interact. This interaction is necessary for transformation – an end to the hostility within us. Relationships with the crucified Lord and with each other provide the foundation for abandoning hatred and embracing healing and unity.

In our Middle Eastern context, as Paul said, we continue to "Preach Christ crucified: a stumbling block to Jews and foolishness to Gentiles" (1 Cor 1:23). Although the majority groups of Muslims and Jews reject the cross, we continue to demonstrate his act of embrace by coming together as believers and embracing one another in reconciliation.

28

Blessing and Cursing

By Salim J. Munayer

In conflict, our first instinct is rarely to bless our enemies. We are not eager to see the other prosper or succeed, and should calamity befall them, we might find it difficult to be sympathetic and may even rejoice.

The subject of blessing and cursing is a strong theme throughout the Bible. A curse comes upon the land because of Adam's disobedience. All of Deuteronomy 27–28 describes how disobedience to God leads to being cursed and faith and obedience bring blessing. The word "blessing" appears more than six hundred times in the Old Testament.

Blessings in the Bible may be described as follows: a blessing is a public declaration of a favored status with God, endowing power for prosperity and success. In all cases, the blessing serves as guide and motivation for pursuing a course of life within the blessing.[1]

Removal from the realm of God's blessing is the result of sin and disobedience to God. In Genesis 3:14, God curses the serpent strongly. In verse 17, God curses the ground because of Adam's sin. Disobedience brings a curse to our land, and the land ceases to be a source of blessing. Our enmity toward people who are created in God's image and likeness also brings a curse upon the land. As written in 2 Chronicles 7:14, "If my people, who are called by my name, will humble themselves and pray and seek my face and turn from their wicked ways, then will I hear from heaven and will forgive their sin and will heal their land." Here, obedience brings healing and blessing to the land.

---

1. Metzger and Coogan, *The Oxford Companion to the Bible*, 92.

In Luke 6:27–28, Jesus talks about blessing as a way to approach our enemies: "But to you who are listening I say: Love your enemies, do good to those who hate you, bless those who curse you, pray for those who mistreat you." As such, blessing is an act of obedience and a foundation for reconciliation.

Blessing and cursing are significant in Middle Eastern cultures as well, in which people have a strong belief in the power of the word, and blessing is built into our languages. When people meet or part, it is with more than "Hello" and includes a blessing of peace – *salaam aleikum* in Arabic; *shalom* in Hebrew. Both the Hebrew and Arabic languages are peppered with phrases of blessing, such as *Allah ya'tik al'afi*, meaning "God give you strength." Blessing and cursing are also intertwined with our religious rituals, such as the tendency to curse our enemies.

At a Musalaha family conference we studied the theme of blessing in the Bible. As we learned and prayed about blessing, the time came to bless one another, and we realized that we were meant to kneel to receive a blessing. In Hebrew, the word for "blessing" is "*bracha*," which shares the root "*berech*" which means "knee." It is humbling to receive a blessing, particularly from someone with whom you are in enmity. By blessing you, that person assumes a higher status. It can be humbling both to bless and to be blessed, and there is considerable vulnerability in the exchange of blessing.

Thus, we understand the significance of blessing in reconciliation. When we bless the "enemy" and pray for their well-being, as Jesus teaches, we are praying that their home and land will be fruitful, and this may be difficult, for we may not want our enemy to succeed and prosper or to be blessed at our expense. It is hard to actively bless someone who contradicts our theological or political principles. Their tribulations or successes may lead us to believe that God is with us or against us, so that the act of blessing requires unselfish giving and confidence that God is in control.

Yet there is great power in blessing. God puts you in a position to affect people's lives through blessing, and this should not be taken lightly. By blessing with the word of God rather than cursing others, we escape a destructive cycle of negative thoughts and revenge and counter the hateful thoughts in our minds and hearts. When you are able to sincerely bless the other, and to receive the other's blessing in return, you will have made a tremendous stride in the process of reconciliation.

Contributors

Rev Dr **Mae Elise Cannon**, born in the United States, is the Executive Director of Churches for Middle East Peace.

Hadassa, who was born in Germany, is married to an Israeli and lives in central Israel with her family. She is a long-time participant in Musalaha activities.

Joshua Korn, a Messianic Jew born in Africa, grew up in Israel. He has worked with Musalaha as a writer, editor, and facilitator, and is now with CURE which runs a network of hospitals in Africa. Josh originally joined CURE as Spiritual Director in Niger.

Salim Munayer, Professor of Theology and Reconciliation, lectures on the subjects both locally and internationally. A Palestinian Christian, he is an Israeli citizen educated in the US, the UK, and Israel. Salim is the founder and director of the Musalaha Ministry of Reconciliation and for the past four decades has been initiating, developing, and implementing Musalaha's unique approach to reconciliation.

Evan Thomas, a Messianic Jew born in New Zealand, immigrated to Israel in the early 1980s. He is pastor of Beit Asaph congregation, a leader of the Messianic Jewish movement, and has been involved with Musalaha from its inception, as well as in reconciliation work with other local and international reconciliation organizations.

Louise Thomsen, born in Denmark, spent time in Israel when her father was part of the Danish clergy there. She led Musalaha's women's activities for nearly a decade.

Bibliography

Arendt, Hannah. *The Human Condition*. Chicago: University of Chicago Press, 1998.

Arnold, Johann Christoph. *Seeking Peace: Notes and Conversations along the Way*. Preface by Thich Nhat Hanh. Farmington: Plough Publishing, 1998.

Ashmore, Richard D., Lee Jussim, and David Wilder, eds. *Social Identity, Intergroup Conflict, and Conflict Reduction*. New York: Oxford University Press, 2001.

Ateek, Naim Stifan. *Justice and Only Justice: A Palestinian Theology of Liberation*. Maryknoll: Orbis Books, 1989.

Augsburger, David. *Caring Enough to Hear and Be Heard*. Ventura, CA: Regal Books, 1982.

———. *Conflict Mediation across Cultures: Pathways and Patterns*. Louisville: Westminster/John Knox Press, 1992.

Bar-On, Dan, and Sami Adwan. "The Psychology of Better Dialogue between Two Separate but Interdependent Narratives." In *Israeli and Palestinian Narratives of Conflict: History's Double Helix*, edited by Robert I. Rotberg, 205–224. Bloomington: Indiana University Press, 2006.

Bar-On, Mordechai. "Conflicting Narratives or Narratives of a Conflict: Can the Zionist and Palestinian Narratives of the 1948 War Be Bridged?" In *Israeli and Palestinian Narratives of Conflict: History's Double Helix*, edited by Robert I. Rotberg, 142–173. Bloomington: Indiana University Press, 2006.

Bar-Tal, Daniel. "Collective Memory of Physical Violence: Its Contribution to the Culture of Violence." In *The Role of Memory in Ethnic Conflict*, edited by E. Cairns and M. D. Roe, 1–29. Houndmills, UK: Palgrave Macmillan, 2003.

———. "From Intractable Conflict through Conflict Resolution to Reconciliation: Psychological Analysis." *Political Psychology* 21, no. 2 (2000): 351–365.

Bar-Tal, Daniel, and Gavriel Salomon. "Israeli-Jewish Narratives of the Israeli-Palestinian Conflict: Evolution, Contents, Functions, and Consequences." In *Israeli and Palestinian Narratives of Conflict: History's Double Helix*, edited by Robert I. Rotberg, 19–46. Bloomington: Indiana University Press, 2006.

Berry, J. W. "Immigration, Acculturation and Adaptation." *Applied Psychology: An International Review* 46 (1997): 5–68.

Boadt, Lawrence. *Jeremiah 1–25*. Wilmington: Michael Glazier, 1982.

Bombay, Amy, Kim Matheson, and Hymie Anisman. "The Impact of Stressors on Second Generation Indian Residential School Survivors." Poster presented at the annual meeting of the National Network for Aboriginal Mental Health Research, Montreal, Quebec, 2008.

———. "Intergenerational Trauma: Convergence of Multiple Processes among First Nations Peoples in Canada." *Journal de la santé autochtone* [Aboriginal Health Journal] (2009): 6–47.

Brewer, Marilynn B. "Ingroup Identification and Intergroup Conflict: When Does Ingroup Love Become Outgroup Hate?" In *Social Identity, Intergroup Conflict, and Conflict Reduction*, edited by Richard D. Ashmore, Lee Jussim, and David Wilder, 24–30. Oxford: Oxford University Press, 2001.

Brueggemann, Walter. *A Commentary of Jeremiah: Exile and Homecoming*. Grand Rapids: Eerdmans, 1998.

Buber, Martin. *A Land of Two Peoples: Martin Buber on Jews and Arabs*, edited by Paul Mendes-Flohr. Chicago: University of Chicago Press, 1983.

Cannon, Mae Elise. *Social Justice Handbook: Small Steps for a Better World*. Downers Grove: InterVarsity Press, 2009.

Ceccarelli, Andrea, and Enrico Molinari. "The Process of Forgiving: Psychological Aspects." *Rivista Di Psicologia Clinica* 3 (2007): 239. Accessed April 8, 2011. http://www.rivistadipsicologiaclinica.it/english/number3_07/Molinari_Ceccarelli.htm.

Clendenen, Avis, and Troy Martin. *Forgiveness: Finding Freedom through Reconciliation*. New York: Crossroad, 2002.

Cloud, Henry. *Changes that Heal*. Grand Rapids: Zondervan, 1992.

Cloud, Henry, and John Townsend. *How People Grow: What the Bible Reveals about Personal Growth*. Grand Rapids: Zondervan, 2001.

Corrie, John. *Dictionary of Mission Theology: Evangelical Foundations*. Nottingham: Inter-Varsity Press, 2007.

Cox, Brian. *Reconciliation Basic Seminar: The Abrahamic Edition*. Santa Barbara: The Reconciliation Institute, 2000.

Currie, Mark. *Postmodern Narrative Theory*. New York: Palgrave, 1998.

Doubilet, Karen. "Coming Together: Theory and Practice of Intergroup Encounters for Palestinians, Arab-Israelis, and Jewish-Israelis." In *Beyond Bullets and Bombs*, edited by Judy Kuriansky, 49–57. Westport, CT: Praeger Publishers, 2007.

Dugan, Maire A. "Prejudice." Beyond Intractability. Conflict Information Consortium, 2004. Accessed April 10, 2011. http://www.beyondintractability.org/essay/prejudice.

Enright, Robert, and Gayle Reed. "Process Model." International Forgiveness Institute. Accessed April 8, 2011. http://www.forgiveness-institute.org/html/process_model.htm.

Eriksen, Thomas Hylland. "Ethnic Identity, National Identity, and Intergroup Conflict: The Significance of Personal Experiences." In *Social Identity, Intergroup Conflict, and Conflict Reduction*, edited by Richard D. Ashmore, Lee Jussim, and David Wilder, 42–68. New York: Oxford University Press, 2001.

Evans-Campbell, T. "Historical Trauma in American Indian/Native Alaska Communities: A Multilevel Framework for Exploring Impacts on Individuals,

Families, and Communities." *Journal of Interpersonal Violence* 23, no. 3 (2008): 316–338.

Fearon, James D. "What Is Identity (as We Now Use the Word)?" Paper submitted at Stanford University, Department of Political Science, November 3, 1999. Accessed April 10, 2011. https://web.stanford.edu/group/fearon-research/cgi-bin/wordpress/wp-content/uploads/2013/10/What-is-Identity-As-we-now-use-the-word-.pdf.

Foster, Roger. "Helping Staff Survivors after Traumatic Event." Unpublished manuscript.

Gowan, Donald D. *Theology in Exodus: Biblical Theology in the Form of a Commentary*. Louisville: Westminster John Knox Press, 1994.

Grimsrud, Ted. "Healing Justice: The Prophet Amos and a 'New' Theology of Justice." In *Peace and Justice Shall Embrace: Power and Theopolitics in the Bible*, edited by Ted Grimsrud and Loren Johns, 64–85. Telford: Pandora Press, 1999.

Halabi, Rabah, and Nava Sonnenschein. "School for Peace: Between Hard Reality and the Jewish-Palestinian Encounters." In *Beyond Bullets and Bombs*, edited by Judy Kuriansky, 277–286. Westport, CT: Praeger Publishers, 2007.

Hanafi, Sari. "Dancing Tango during Peacebuilding: Palestinian-Israeli People-to-People Programs for Conflict Resolution." In *Beyond Bullets and Bombs*, edited by Judy Kuriansky, 69–79. Westport, CT: Praeger Publishers, 2007.

Hanke, Katja, and Ronald Fischer. "Socioeconomical and Sociopolitical Correlates of Interpersonal Forgiveness: A Three-Level Meta-Analysis of the Enright Forgiveness Inventory across 13 Societies." International Journal of Psychology 48, no. 4 (2013): 514–526. https://doi.org/10.1080/00207594.2011.651086.

Heraclitus: The Complete Fragments: Translation and Commentary and the Greek Text. Translated by William Harris. Middlebury College, 1994. http://wayback.archive-it.org/6670/20161201175137/http://community.middlebury.edu/~harris/Philosophy/heraclitus.pdf.

Horenczyk, Gabriel. "Minorities and Intergroup Contact: Conceptualizations and Findings." Lecture presentation at annual meeting of Musalaha board and staff in Jerusalem, February 2010.

Huo, Yuen J., Heather J. Smith, Tom R. Tyler, and E. Allan Lind. "Superordinate Identification, Subgroup Identification, and Justice Concerns: Is Separatism the Problem; Is Assimilation the Answer?" *American Psychological Society* 7, no. 1 (January 1996), 40–45.

Jones, L. Gregory. *Embodying Forgiveness: A Theological Analysis*. Grand Rapids: Eerdmans, 1995.

Jordan, S., K. Matheson, and H. Anisman. "Supportive and Unsupportive Social Interactions in Relation to Cultural Adaptation and Psychological Distress among Somali Refugees Exposed to Collective or Interpersonal Traumas." *Journal of Cross-Cultural Psychology* 40, no. 5 (September 2009): 853–874.

Juster, Dan. "A Messianic Jew Looks at the Land Promises." In *The Land Cries Out: Theology of the Land in the Israeli-Palestinian Context*, edited by Lisa Loden and Salim J. Munayer, 63–81. Eugene: Wipf & Stock, 2011.

Kelman, Herbert C. "The Role of National Identity in Conflict Resolution: Experiences from Israeli-Palestinian Problem-Solving Workshops." In *Social Identity, Intergroup Conflict, and Conflict Resolution*, edited by Richard D. Ashmore, Lee Jussim, and David Wilder, 187–212. New York: Oxford University Press, 2001.

King, Coretta Scott. "Introduction." In *Strength to Love*, by Martin Luther King Jr. Philadelphia: Augsburg Fortress, 1981.

Kotter, John. *Leading Change*. Boston: Harvard Business School Press, 1996.

Kraft, Charles. *Anthropology for Christian Witness*. Maryknoll: Orbis, 1996.

Kraybill, Ron. "The Cycle of Reconciliation." In *Seeking and Pursuing Peace: The Process, the Pain, and the Product*, edited by Salim J. Munayer, 73–78. Jerusalem: Musalaha, 1998.

Kruschwitz, Robert B. "Why Should We Forgive?" In *Christian Reflection: A Series in Faith and Ethics*, edited by Robert Kruschwitz, 4–18. Baylor University: Center for Christian Ethics, 2001.

Kupermintz, Haggai, and Gavriel Saloman. "Lessons to Be Learned from Research on Peace Education in the Context of Intractable Conflict." *Theory into Practice* 44, no. 4 (2005): 293–302.

Lederach, John Paul. *Building Peace: Sustainable Reconciliation in Divided Societies*. Washington, DC: United States Institute of Peace Press, 1997.

———. *The Journey toward Reconciliation*. Scottdale, PA: Herald Press, 1999.

Lencioni, Patrick. *Five Dysfunctions of a Team: A Leadership Fable*. San Francisco: Jossey-Bass, 2002.

MacIntyre, Alasdair. *After Virtue: A Study in Moral Theory*. Notre Dame: University of Notre Dame Press, 1984.

Marshall, Christopher. *Beyond Retribution: A New Testament Vision for Justice, Crime, and Punishment*. Grand Rapids: Eerdmans, 2001.

Metzger, Bruce M., and Michael D. Coogan, eds. *The Oxford Companion to the Bible*. New York: Oxford University Press, 1993.

Munayer, Salim J. "The Ethnic Identity of Palestinian Arab Christian Adolescents in Israel." PhD diss., University of Wales, 2000.

Myers, Ched, and Elaine Enns. *Ambassadors of Reconciliation: New Testament Reflections on Restorative Justice and Peacemaking*. Vol. 1. Maryknoll: Orbis, 2009.

Nouwen, Henri. *Life of the Beloved: Spiritual Living in a Secular World*. New York: Crossroad Publishing, 1992

O'Donovan, Oliver. *The Ways of Judgment*. Grand Rapids: Eerdmans, 2005.

Open Doors International. Lecture on Intergenerational Trauma, December 28–30, 2013.

The Open University. "What Is Identity: Questions of Identity." OpenLearn. Accessed April 11, 2011. http://openlearn.open.ac.uk/mod/oucontent/view.php?id=399036&section=1.1.

Pappe, Ilan. "The Bridging Narrative Concept." In *Israeli and Palestinian Narratives of Conflict: History's Double Helix*, edited by Robert I. Rotberg, 194–204. Bloomington: Indiana University Press, 2006.

Philpot, Catherine. "Forgiveness: Definitions and Effects." In *Forgiveness: A Sampling of Research Results*, 5–7. Washington, DC: Office of International Affairs, 2008.

Philpot, Catherine, and Matthew Hornsey. "Asking Forgiveness for the Sins of Many: Does it Work?" In *Forgiveness: A Sampling of Research Results*, 28–30. Washington, DC: Office of International Affairs, 2008.

Prince, Robert. "Historical Trauma: Psychohistorical Reflections on the Holocaust." In *Children Surviving Persecution: An International Study of Trauma and Healing*, edited by J. Kestenberg and C. Kahn, 43–55. Westport, CT: Praeger, 1998.

Regehr, Keith Allen. "Justice and Forgiveness: Restorative Justice Practice and the Recovery of Theological Memory." PhD diss., University of Waterloo, Ontario, Canada, 2007.

Reychler, Luc, and Thania Paffenholz. *Peacebuilding: A Field Guide*. Boulder: Lynne Rienner Publishers, 2001.

Rimmon-Kenan, Shlomith. "Concepts of Narrative." *Collegium: Studies across Disciplines in the Humanities and Social Sciences* 1 (2006): 10–19.

Rotberg, Robert I. "Building Legitimacy through Narrative." In *Israeli and Palestinian Narratives of Conflict: History's Double Helix*, edited by Robert I. Rotberg, 1–18. Bloomington: Indiana University Press, 2006.

———. "Preface" to *Israeli and Palestinian Narratives of Conflict: History's Double Helix*, edited by Robert I. Rotberg. Bloomington: Indiana University Press, 2006.

Rye, Mark S., Dawn M. Loiacono, Chad D. Folck, Brandon T. Olszewski, Todd A. Heim, and Benjamin P. Madia. "Evaluation of the Psychometric Properties of Two Forgiveness Scales." *Current Psychology* 20, no. 3 (Spring 2001): 260–277.

Smith, Barbara Herrnstein. "Narrative Versions, Narrative Theories." In *On Narrative*, edited by W. J. T. Mitchell, 209–232. Chicago: University of Chicago Press, 1981.

Staub, Ervin, and Laurie Anne Pearlman. "Promoting Reconciliation and Forgiveness after Mass Violence: Rwanda and Other Settings." In *Forgiveness: A Sampling of Research Results*, 31–34. Washington, DC: Office of International Affairs, 2008.

Steinberg, Shoshana, and Dan Bar-On. "Dialogue in the Midst of an Ongoing Conflict: A Group Process of Israeli Jewish and Palestinian Students." In *Beyond Bullets and Bombs*, edited by Judy Kuriansky, 139–150. Westport, CT: Praeger Publishers, 2007.

Stephan, Walter G., and Cookie W. Stephan. *Intergroup Relations*. Social Psychology Series, edited by John Harvey. Madison: Brown & Benchmark Publishers, 1996.

Subkoviak, Michael J., Robert D. Enright, Ching-Ru Wu, Elizabeth A. Gassin, Suzanne Freedman, Leanne M. Olson and Issidoros Sarinopoulos. "Measuring

Interpersonal Forgiveness in Late Adolescence and Middle Adulthood." *Journal of Adolescence* 18 (1995): 641–655.

Teaching Tolerance. "Test Yourself for Hidden Bias." Southern Poverty Law Center, 2020. https://www.tolerance.org/professional-development/test-yourself-for-hidden-bias.

Toews, John E. *Romans: Believers Church Bible Commentary*. Scottdale, PA: Herald Press, 2004.

Volf, Miroslav. *The End of Memory: Remembering Rightly in a Violent World*. Grand Rapids: Eerdmans, 2006.

———. *Exclusion and Embrace: A Theological Exploration of Identity, Otherness, and Reconciliation*. Nashville: Abingdon, 1996.

Wallis, Jim. *God's Politics: Why the American Right Gets It Wrong and the Left Doesn't Get It*. Oxford: Lion Book, 2005.

Wesley-Esquimaux, Cynthia C., and Magdalena Smolewski. *Historic Trauma and Aboriginal Healing*. The Aboriginal Healing Foundation Research Series. Ottawa: Aboriginal Healing Foundation, 2004.

White, Hayden. *Figural Realism: Studies in the Mimesis Effect*. Baltimore: Johns Hopkins University Press, 1999.

MUSALAHA
מוסאלחה • مصالحة

Based in Jerusalem, Musalaha is a non-profit organization that promotes and facilitates reconciliation between Israelis and Palestinians from diverse ethnic and religious backgrounds. For those who have a common faith, we advocate and facilitate reconciliation encounters among Israeli and Palestinian believers based on the life and teaching of Jesus. Within the wider community, we seek to impact our societies through building bridges among Muslims, Christians, and Jews according to the Abrahamic moral principles contained in all three faiths. Musalaha, which means "reconciliation" in Arabic, was founded in 1990.

Based on our nearly thirty years of experience in facilitating reconciliation, we developed a "Curriculum of Reconciliation" which embraces our vision and understanding of reconciliation and characterizes our methodology of interpersonal and intergroup approaches to conflict.

www.musalaha.org

Langham

Langham Literature and its imprints are a ministry of Langham Partnership.

Langham Partnership is a global fellowship working in pursuit of the vision God entrusted to its founder John Stott –

> *to facilitate the growth of the church in maturity and Christ-likeness through raising the standards of biblical preaching and teaching.*

Our vision is to see churches in the Majority World equipped for mission and growing to maturity in Christ through the ministry of pastors and leaders who believe, teach and live by the word of God.

Our mission is to strengthen the ministry of the word of God through:
- nurturing national movements for biblical preaching
- fostering the creation and distribution of evangelical literature
- enhancing evangelical theological education

especially in countries where churches are under-resourced.

Our ministry

Langham Preaching partners with national leaders to nurture indigenous biblical preaching movements for pastors and lay preachers all around the world. With the support of a team of trainers from many countries, a multi-level programme of seminars provides practical training, and is followed by a programme for training local facilitators. Local preachers' groups and national and regional networks ensure continuity and ongoing development, seeking to build vigorous movements committed to Bible exposition.

Langham Literature provides Majority World preachers, scholars and seminary libraries with evangelical books and electronic resources through publishing and distribution, grants and discounts. The programme also fosters the creation of indigenous evangelical books in many languages, through writer's grants, strengthening local evangelical publishing houses, and investment in major regional literature projects, such as one volume Bible commentaries like *The Africa Bible Commentary* and *The South Asia Bible Commentary*.

Langham Scholars provides financial support for evangelical doctoral students from the Majority World so that, when they return home, they may train pastors and other Christian leaders with sound, biblical and theological teaching. This programme equips those who equip others. Langham Scholars also works in partnership with Majority World seminaries in strengthening evangelical theological education. A growing number of Langham Scholars study in high quality doctoral programmes in the Majority World itself. As well as teaching the next generation of pastors, graduated Langham Scholars exercise significant influence through their writing and leadership.

To learn more about Langham Partnership and the work we do visit **langham.org**